Praise for *The AI Imper*

"This book is compelling and a must read for not only CEO's but for anyone in a Technology Leadership position. The history, review of types or AI, and most important - step-by-step guide on how to implement and measure ROI. Fantastic read!"

Cheryl Moody
CEO GoCIO.net

"This book is a deep dive into the AI evolution, packing historical insights with a roadmap on responsible AI utilization. Its straight talk on ethical AI progression and hands-on prompt engineering techniques hit the mark for any leader looking to drive meaningful AI integration. It underscores a collaborative stance, transparency, and ethical coding—key for CEOs navigating the AI terrain. The broad-spectrum case studies and actionable advice on fine-tuning large language models like GPT make it a go-to resource for guiding organizations responsibly and creatively into the AI-enhanced future."

Patrick Patterson
CEO Level Agency

"This book was very helpful in enhancing my understanding of the morass of AI. Even the highly technical topics are broken down in a way that kept me engaged. This is a must read!"

Malinda Passmore
Founder Maximum Possibilities LLC

"This is a must-read primer for CEOs who need to make better decisions about how and when to use AI. It walks you through the principles and applications with knowledge of an engineer presented with the focus of a CEO."

Scott Levy
CEO ResultMaps.com

"As someone who works closely with AI implementation, I found the book *The AI Imperative* to be a valuable resource. John Arnott's comprehensive approach to measuring AI ROI is impressive. From infrastructure costs to intangible benefits, the holistic approach he proposes allows for a nuanced evaluation of AI's impact on business performance. He reminds us that investing in AI is not a one-off deal but a sustained commitment to adaptation and growth. This book is a must-read for anyone navigating the AI landscape— it offers more than just insights, it offers a roadmap to success. Five out of five stars."

George Mayfield
CEO, Frameworks Consortium

"*The AI Imperative: A CEO's Playbook for Enterprise Artificial Intelligence* by John Arnott II is a well-crafted broad and deep overall for any professional in today's market. Each chapter provides a tour of both the practical commercial use and the nuts and bolts back end of how AI can and should be embedded into any organization. I am not a technology professional by training yet, felt myself pulled into understanding the use and workflow of AI in different scenarios. "Playbook" is the right description of this text; I am not sure if the author used AI to come up with that name but it's spot on. The AI Imperative is much more than what we have been feed by the latest and greatest "thought leadership" on the web but rather it is a well-designed reference guide that tells a story of how to develop a process to apply AI from decision making tools to content development in an immediate but careful manner."

Daniel Torpey
Partner – Ernst & Young, LLP

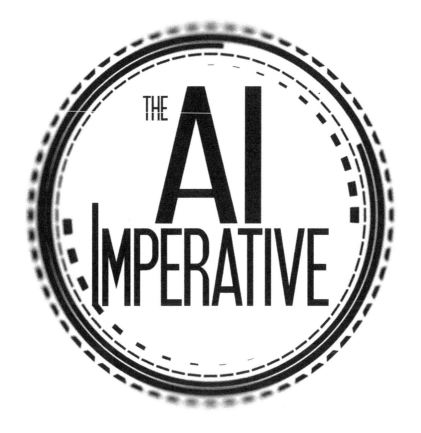

THE AI IMPERATIVE

A CEO's Playbook for Enterprise Artificial Intelligence

JOHN ARNOTT, II

Performance Publishing Group
McKinney, TX

ISBN: 978-1-961781-22-1 Hardback
978-1-961781-06-1 Paperback

PERFORMANCE
PUBLISHING

THE AI IMPERATIVE

A CEO's Playbook for Enterprise Artificial Intelligence

JOHN ARNOTT, II

Contents

Preface

I AM THRILLED TO SHARE this book on implementing AI in corporations, the culmination of years of research and real-world experience. My goal is to provide executives with practical guidance on harnessing AI's transformative potential.

I am deeply grateful to the many collaborators who enriched this book's contents, especially my parents John and Ellen, whose wisdom and encouragement motivated me throughout this journey. My wife Daisy provided valuable feedback on drafts and was a pillar of support. My sister Michelle offered guidance on the publishing process and industry insights despite her demanding schedule. Their contributions were truly invaluable. I would also like to express my sincere appreciation to Doug King and Eleanor Patrick at ContentFirst.Marketing for their tireless efforts and expertise in making this book a reality.

It is my sincere hope that this book serves as a strategic guide for enterprises seeking to successfully unlock the many benefits of AI. While adopting AI comes with challenges, I firmly believe that organizations who embrace this technology thoughtfully and responsibly will gain a sustained competitive advantage. I welcome your feedback on applying the frameworks outlined in this book within your enterprise.

Let us continue learning together and shaping the responsible path forward for AI. I wish you the very best in leveraging AI to drive innovation, efficiency, and resounding success in your organization.

With gratitude,

John Arnott, II
John@JohnArnott.com
www.JohnArnott.com/AIimperative

November 15, 2023

Introduction
The Journey of Innovation: My Pursuit of AI

Once upon a time, in the small but bustling town of Austin, Texas, a curious young man embarked on a journey that would not only change his life but also potentially alter the trajectory of many future businesses. That curious young man was me.

The year was 1986. The cold war was nearing its end, Microsoft was rising to prominence, and I was about to enter the University of Texas to study computer science. A profound fascination with the infinite possibilities of artificial intelligence had already taken root in my mind. I dreamed of creating machines that could think, learn, and solve complex problems. I yearned to turn science fiction into reality.

At The University, I discovered Prolog, a rules-based AI programming language known for its prowess in computational linguistics. Intrigued by the potential, I spent countless hours in my dorm room experimenting with its logical rules and constructing intricate solutions to complex problems. Yet, Prolog was only a window into the broader, rapidly-evolving realm of AI.

In 1988, during my Junior year, I encountered my first AI class. It was an opportunity to learn LISP programming. LISP, an acronym for List Processing, was one of the oldest high-level programming languages, primarily designed for artificial intelligence research. Its unique features, such as the capability to modify its own code and the dynamic creation of new objects, had a profound impact on my understanding of AI. I marveled at how LISP, with its powerful abstraction and metaprogramming capabilities, could simulate intelligent behavior.

But as I delved deeper, I noticed an unsettling reality. While the theoretical aspects of AI were captivating, the practical applications were not quite ready for the business world. The technology was embryonic, the implementations were cumbersome, and the commercial prospects seemed far-fetched. I realized I needed to pivot. I decided to leverage my knowledge of technology to help businesses grow.

It turned out the timing was great. The late 80s were the beginning of what would be known as "The Second AI Winter".

I dedicated the next few decades of my life to growing businesses, intertwining emerging technologies with business needs, and guiding companies toward digital transformation. However, the seed of artificial intelligence sown in my heart during the college years never stopped growing.

In 2018, I observed that AI was beginning to evolve at an unprecedented pace. Deep learning algorithms were making breakthroughs, data was becoming the new oil, and the dream of creating intelligent machines seemed closer to reality. My entrepreneurial spirit lit up again, sensing a sea change on the horizon.

By 2021, I saw an opportunity to marry AI with my digital marketing company, ContentFirst.Marketing. I envisaged using AI to drive search engine optimization and content creation. Leveraging natural language processing algorithms, I imagined creating persuasive marketing content, optimizing it to rank high in search engines, and thereby driving more traffic to my clients' websites. The idea was ambitious, but I was ready to take the plunge.

Two years later, in 2023, my vision had come to fruition. AI had matured to a level where it could drive tangible business benefits. After years of anticipation and perseverance, I could finally fulfill my dream of helping businesses embrace artificial intelligence. The journey was long and arduous yet incredibly fulfilling.

My tale is a testament to the relentless pursuit of innovation. It's a story of a dream conceived in the classrooms of the University of Texas, nurtured through decades of technological evolution, and realized at the crossroads of artificial intelligence and digital marketing. And even though this vision had finally materialized, I knew this was merely the beginning. As AI continued to evolve, I was ready to ride the wave, turning every crest into an opportunity and every trough into a lesson. After all, the man who dreams of the future is the one who shapes it.

Welcome to a transformative journey into Artificial Intelligence that is poised to revolutionize the way businesses operate and empower their knowledge workers. In this book, we will explore how integrating AI into the enterprise can elevate productivity, efficiency, and innovation to drive unprecedented business growth.

As organizations embrace the potential of AI, the role of prompt engineering emerges as a critical catalyst. It serves as a conduit to harness the power of large language models and unleash the creativity and ingenuity of knowledge workers. By crafting well-designed prompts, businesses can empower their workforce to interact seamlessly with AI systems, unlocking new levels of productivity and efficiency.

Through the strategic integration of prompt engineering, businesses can streamline their operations, automate repetitive tasks, and unleash the potential for new sources of innovation and creativity. By augmenting the capabilities of knowledge workers and enabling them to collaborate with intelligent systems, organizations can foster a culture of continuous improvement and push the boundaries of what is possible.

In this book, we will delve into the intricacies of prompt engineering within the enterprise context. We will explore practical techniques, case studies, and best practices that demonstrate how businesses can leverage these approaches to transform their operations. By embracing AI-powered prompt engineering, organizations can not only unlock new insights to drive informed decision-making but also, propel themselves toward sustainable growth and success.

Get ready to embark on a journey that combines the powerful synergy of prompt engineering, AI, and the enterprising spirit. Together, let's unlock a future where businesses thrive by leveraging the full potential of AI and empowering their knowledge workers to shape a world of innovation, efficiency, and unprecedented growth.

The Evolution of Artificial Intelligence: A Historical Exploration

THE REALM OF ARTIFICIAL INTELLIGENCE (AI) is an intriguing sphere that has significantly grown and expanded over the years. This fascinating world isn't confined to the science fictions we grew up marveling at, but rather, it has become a groundbreaking reality that continues to reshape various aspects of our world today. From self-driving cars and voice-activated personal assistants to barcode scanners and recommendation algorithms, AI technologies have demonstrated their vast potential by seamlessly integrating into our everyday lives.

We live in an era of rapid technological advancement where AI is no longer just an intriguing prospect for the future, but an innovative force dominating the present. As AI continues to evolve, it becomes increasingly important to understand not just its functionalities and capabilities, but also its origins and the distinctive historical journey that has crafted its current form. Looking back through history, we trace this path back to the rudimentary beginnings that sparked the idea and evolution of AI.

From the first conceptualization of automated machines to the development of machine learning and neural networks, we dive into this captivating exploration that unearths AI's roots and history. The journey takes us across various milestones and breakthroughs, proffers a glance at significant leaps in the field, and presents insights into the roles and contributions of visionary scientists and researchers along the way. We delve into contextual explorations of how these critical aspects of AI have profoundly impacted society, industries, economies, and our lives.

By embarking on this intriguing exploration of AI's history and understanding its genesis, we gain a comprehensive overview of the revolutionary technology and its phenomenal rise. As we traverse through time, we grasp how artificial intelligence emerged as a transformative power and continues to influence and shape our future.

This comprehensive historical exploration of AI, therefore, provides a timeline and context that helps us make sense of the present and anticipate the future.

Early Origins

The genesis of AI as a concept has deep and firmly rooted connections that reach back into the annals of history and mythology. The concept of artificial beings or automatons, imbued with intelligence or whimsy, was a recurring theme in ancient stories and folklore, illustrating the deep-seated human fascination with creating artificial life. Legend tells us of enchanting tales of metallic gods and artificial servants, exhibiting complex functioning which is likened to modern AI.

However, despite these early imaginations, the first scientific seeds of what we would come to recognize as modern AI were only sown in the well-documented scientific studies of the 20th century. The early 20th century brought with it a set of influential figures who would come to lay the groundwork for AI – and amongst them, Alan Turing stands out as an exceptional mind and visionary.

Alan Turing – often hailed as the father of modern computer science – played an indispensable role in the history of Artificial Intelligence. His pioneering work synthesized and unified laws of computation that would eventually shape the landscape of AI. Turing's seminal work was encapsulated in the concept of the 'Turing machine' he introduced in the mid-1930s. This theoretical machine was conceived to simulate the logic of any computer algorithm, no matter how complex. That construct is paramount to the functioning of modern computers and marks an early stride towards the dream of artificial intelligence.

Several years later, Turing introduced to the world another fundamental concept pertaining to AI – the renowned 'Turing test.' The Turing test, published in his 1950 paper "Computing Machinery and Intelligence", was devised as a criterion to determine a machine's ability to exhibit intelligent behavior equivalent to, or indistinguishable from, that of a human. If a machine could convincingly simulate human conversation without the evaluator distinguishing it from a human response, it could be deemed to possess artificial intelligence. The Turing test still holds theoretical significance and remains a topic of scrutiny and discussion among researchers, marking a vital early step towards defining and recognizing the concept of artificial intelligence.

Thus, while humans have been dreaming about artificial intelligence for centuries, the inception of modern AI is intricately linked with the work of a handful of visionaries like Alan Turing. They paved the path for today's era of advanced AI, and their revolutionary ideas continue to influence and drive the AI technology of the present and future.

The Birth of AI

Historians often pinpoint the year 1956 as the birth year of Artificial Intelligence, a turning point from where the science-fiction trope of thinking machines began its transition into concrete scientific pursuit. It was in this year that the term "Artificial Intelligence" was first officially used during the now-famous Dartmouth Conference, held at Dartmouth College in Hanover, New Hampshire.

John McCarthy, a young Assistant Professor of Mathematics at Dartmouth at the time, along with the brilliant Marvin Minsky, Nathaniel Rochester, and Claude Shannon, were the lynchpins behind this groundbreaking conference. McCarthy is often attributed with the introduction of the term 'Artificial Intelligence', a choice aptly encapsulating the essence of their scientific pursuit – to mirror and replicate human intelligence within a machine.

Their proposal for the conference was revolutionary, stating, "every aspect of learning or any other feature of intelligence can in principle be so precisely described that a machine can be made to simulate it." This bold assertion signaled an innovative shift in technological and scientific thought, laying the groundworks for formalizing the concepts and methods of what is now encompassed under the vast umbrella of AI.

The same Marvin Minsky from the early days of AI went on to co-found the Massachusetts Institute of Technology's Media Lab and author significant works that profoundly shaped the AI field. Nathaniel Rochester, one of IBM's earliest employees, significantly contributed to computer design and AI research. And Claude Shannon, often dubbed the 'father of information theory', laid the groundwork for digital circuit design theory.

These pioneers passionately believed in the incredible potential and possibility of AI, providing a fresh, architectural blueprint for a new branch of computer science. They dared to envision a future where machines could solve problems reserved for humans, manipulating data and symbols to mimic the processes of human thought. The Dartmouth Conference and the propositions put forward by these forefathers of AI signaled the dawn of an ambitious new era of science and technology – the era of Artificial Intelligence. As such, the year 1956 is celebrated among many as the genesis of AI, marking a crucial juncture in mankind's technological evolution.

Automated Machines and Early AI

The 1960s marked a time of enthusiastic exploration in the sphere of Artificial Intelligence. Bolstered by the momentum generated at the Dartmouth conference, AI research was entering its first golden age. This period saw vast investment in AI projects, a rapid growth in AI researchers, and notable technical achievements that paved the path we see today.

A significant stride during this period was the opening of the first-ever AI laboratory at the Massachusetts Institute of Technology (MIT) in 1959. Marvin Minsky, one of the Dartmouth conference's key figures, along with his colleague John McCarthy, was instrumental in setting up this lab. The lab, which later came to be known as the MIT Computer Science and Artificial Intelligence Laboratory, became a hub of innovation and a fantastic breeding ground for AI ideas. It played a pivotal role in many breakthroughs to come.

In parallel, significant progress was made in the field of language recognition programs. Leading the way was the work of Joseph Weizenbaum, a German-American Computer Scientist and a prominent figure in the early days of AI research. Weizenbaum shot to fame in the mid-1960s with the creation of ELIZA, a computer program designed to simulate conversation with human users.

ELIZA, built at the MIT AI lab, was a monumental moment in AI history. It sparked considerable intrigue and excitement due to its ability to mirror human-like conversation by recognizing keywords and phrases, then generating seemingly thoughtful responses. While ELIZA did not truly understand conversation like a human, the illusion of understanding left many users astounded – and highlighted the potential that AI held.

ELIZA is often considered one of the earliest efforts at creating what we would today refer to as a 'chatbot' – laying the groundwork for contemporary AI applications such as Siri, Alexa, and Google Assistant. It's recognition capabilities opened up the realm of possibilities for future machine-human interaction.

Thus, the 1960s marked a crucial phase in the timeline of AI. The pioneering efforts of researchers and scientists, particularly at institutions like

MIT, set the stage for the blossoming of AI as a scientific discipline, shaping the direction of this field for years to come. They showcased the transformative potentials of AI, painting a compelling image of the technological marvels that lay ahead.

Revolution of AI

To journey through the history of AI is to witness a myriad of inventive breakthroughs and notable milestones. One such landmark was the creation of LISP, a programming language, developed by John McCarthy in 1958. LISP, short for 'LISt Processing', emerged as the preferred coding language for AI research and still holds significance in the AI realm today.

LISP was the first of its kind to support the conditional expressions and recursion necessary for AI computations. Its high-level functionalities granted researchers the ability to tackle abstract AI problems more directly and without worrying too much about the underlying hardware. Hence, LISP's unique aspects contributed significantly to accelerating progress in AI research and development and fostered meaningful advances such as machine learning and problem-solving.

In the early 1970s, another influential programming language, Prolog, was developed by Alain Colmerauer and his team. Short for 'PROgrammation en LOGique,' Prolog became closely associated with AI research due to its focus on symbolic reasoning, a central aspect of many AI applications. Like LISP, Prolog simplified the problem-solving process, allowing AI researchers to express complex ideas efficiently and fundamentally changing the path of AI programming.

Progressing towards the 1980s, AI research achieved another significant breakthrough with the advent of 'expert systems.' An expert system encapsulates the knowledge of domain experts in a specific field and applies it to problem-solving, decision-making, or giving advice. These systems incorporated logic and rules to make informed decisions much like a human expert. They notably found applications in areas such as diagnosis in medicine, process control in industries, and financial forecasting.

Expert systems also represented a major leap into real-world applications, demonstrating that AI could not just replicate human intelligence but provide valuable insights and solutions in complex, real-life situations. They provided a glimpse into a future where machines would take an active role in decision-making, drastically transforming industries and redefining jobs requiring expert knowledge.

The revolutionary efforts of AI pioneers such as McCarthy and Colmerauer, and the introduction of technologies like expert systems, showcase the rapid and impressive evolution of AI technology. Tracing this historical journey brings to light the relentless ventures and inventions that have shaped AI into what we witness today – and set the stage for subsequent breakthroughs and advancements.

Modern AI

As the curtain rose on the 21st century, the field of AI had expanded beyond lab experiments and into various facets of everyday life. The dawn of this new era heralded an age of far-reaching advancements and innovation, leading to AI's permeation and substantial impact across various industries such as healthcare, finance, and entertainment.

The healthcare industry, for example, started harnessing AI capabilities in a multitude of roles, from predicting patient risks and offering personalized medicine to aiding in radiology and surgery with machine precision and intelligence. In finance, AI powered algorithms for predictive analysis, high-frequency trading, and fraud detection, transforming the industry landscape. In the entertainment sector, AI played a crucial role in personalizing content, creating special effects, and even composing music.

One of the primary factors spearheading this rapid advancement in AI during the turn of the millennium was the advent of big data. With the internet and technology boom, an enormous amount of data was being generated every second. This big data, when harnessed correctly, provided AI systems with an unprecedented amount of information to learn from, enabling more accurate predictions, better decision-making, and more efficient operations.

Alongside all this, machine learning – a subset of AI – emerged as a cornerstone in the research and development of AI technology. Machine learning algorithms use statistical techniques to enable AI systems to learn and improve from experience, just as a human being would. This gave birth to innovative applications like Google's search algorithms, Facebook's personalized news feeds, and Amazon's product recommendations that we see and interact with in our daily lives.

Neural networks added another dimension to the expanding AI universe. Inspired by the biological neural networks of the human brain, they revolutionize the way machines interpret and understand data. They have been instrumental in the success of advanced AI systems, including breakthrough technologies like virtual assistants such as Siri, Alexa, and Google Assistant, and autonomous vehicles.

These virtual assistants epitomize modern AI's capabilities to understand and respond to human language accurately, making everyday tasks more manageable. And autonomous driving vehicles, another fantastic stride in AI, depict a future on the horizon where machines take over complex human tasks like driving.

As we turned the corner into the 21st century, it became obvious that the AI landscape had undergone a seismic shift. Powered by innovations in big data, machine learning, and neural networks, AI had transitioned from an experimental concept to a practical solution with tangible impacts across various industries. This period therefore marked a transformative era in the history of AI, painting a vibrant picture of how far AI had come and the boundless potential it held for the future.

Future of AI

AI's incredible journey from an intriguing concept to a technological reality has been truly transformative, shaping society and industry in countless ways. As we peer into the future, we stand on the cusp of an era where humans and AI coexist and complement each other, dynamically accelerating progress and innovation.

One of the captivating predictions for the future revolves around an era of 'superintelligence.' This hypothesized concept suggests the creation of machines that surpass human beings in almost all economically valuable work. Such a scenario would entail radical changes to our society as AI becomes an integral part of every sector and industry, leading to enhanced efficiency, productivity, and decision-making.

However, there is considerable debate and anticipation around this potential future. Some envision a utopian scenario where superintelligent AI helps us solve complex global issues like climate change, disease eradication, poverty reduction, and more. These optimists imagine AI doing more than mimicking human intelligence, leveraging expansive data and unparalleled processing speeds to find solutions that humans haven't yet conceived.

On the other hand, other experts cautiously warn about the potential ethical, social, and economic implications. There are concerns about job displacement due to automation, privacy issues, and unchecked AI systems' potential to cause unintended harm. These fears underscore the need for robust ethical and regulatory frameworks as we navigate towards this revolutionary future.

Aside from superintelligence, the future of AI holds immense promise in areas such as healthcare, education, transportation, space exploration, and more. We are already seeing AI algorithms detecting diseases earlier than ever before, self-driving cars taking to the roads, and AI-powered robots helping in distant space missions. The evolving synergy of AI in such diverse applications indicates a future where AI will significantly shape humanity's path and our relationship with technology.

The theme of AI's future is predominantly one of positive anticipation mingled with cautious introspection. As we move towards this future, it becomes essential to foster responsible AI development, learning from the past and present to ensure that the future of AI aligns with the broader interests of humanity. Thus, while the tremendous possibilities of AI capture our imagination, the journey ahead asks us to tread with responsibility, foresight, and consideration for the profound impact AI will have on the fabric of society.

Conclusion

As we draw the curtains on this in-depth journey through the past, present, and conjectured future of AI, we realize that the evolution witnessed is nothing short of remarkable. What began as a concept in the realms of mythology and science fiction has today evolved into a technological phenomenon, fundamentally reshaping the world as we know it.

The conjured images of artificial beings and 'thinking machines' from our shared cultural imaginations have given way to a reality where AI is ubiquitous. Today, AI infiltrates almost every facet of our lives, from personal virtual assistants and recommendation algorithms to cutting-edge research in healthcare, finance, and more. Our venture into the AI landscape, traversing through its origins, bright milestones, transformative breakthroughs, and the luminous personas who fueled its progress, has been a truly enlightening exploration.

Undeniably, the journey of AI has been a testament to human ingenuity and persistence. Each shift, each advancement – from Alan Turing's foundational work, the birth of AI at the Dartmouth Conference, to the advent of machine learning and neural networks – has been a building block that has shaped AI's current form.

But the voyage is far from over. AI is not a static field. It is vibrant and ceaselessly innovative, continually evolving to push the boundaries of what technology can accomplish. In a world ceaselessly hungry for advancement, businesses and individuals alike are increasingly leveraging AI, fueling its growth, and revealing new possibilities.

As we stand on the verge of a new era where superintelligence and cohabitation with AI might become our new reality, we look forward with a mix of anticipation and responsibility. We recognize that with tremendous power comes the demand equally for careful deliberation, ethical programming, and regulatory scrutiny.

Despite the uncertainties that the future may hold, one thing remains indisputable: AI has transformed and will continue to redefine the way we interact with the world. In the light of such transformative potential and influence, the importance of understanding AI's history and its trajectory becomes even more vital, ensuring that as we forge ahead, we do so with informed minds and considerate actions.

So, as we conclude this exploration, we acknowledge that we stand not at the end but in the midst of a grand journey as AI continues to evolve and shape our future.

It's quite the tale, one of continuous learning, constant breakthrough, and stunning potential, and one that we are all actively contributing to as we move forward into the exciting realm of the unknown. AI has undoubtedly come a long way, but in many ways, it's journey and ours with it is just beginning.

What is Generative AI?

ARTIFICIAL INTELLIGENCE HAS EVOLVED from simply analyzing data to now being able to autonomously create new data and content. This generative capability is driving transformations across industries. In this chapter, we will dive into understanding what generative AI is, how it works, the state-of-the-art techniques behind it, and its diverse current and potential applications.

Generative AI refers broadly to AI systems that can produce novel, high-quality artifacts like images, video, text, code, designs, and more from scratch. Unlike traditional, manually programmed software, generative AI relies on machine learning to train models on large datasets until they can generate new data similar to what they have seen before. The outputs are unique, realistic, and often indistinguishable from content created by humans.

From deepfakes to AI-written essays and music, generative AI is making tremendous strides. Under the hood, approaches like generative adversarial networks, variational autoencoders, diffusion models, reinforcement learning, and transformer neural networks (which we'll look at in a moment) enable the modeling of complex distributions in data to create new examples from them. The applications of these approaches span content creation, process automation, augmenting human creativity, and more.

However, there are rising concerns regarding potential misuse and biases perpetuated by generative AI. As AI's capabilities continue to rapidly advance, it is crucial we work towards developing ethical, transparent, and controlled frameworks for generative models.

In this chapter, we will do a deep dive into how generative AI works, the key technologies powering it, where it is headed, and how we can steer progress responsibly. Let's get started!

Generative AI refers to artificial intelligence systems that can generate new content and artifacts that are novel, high-quality, and realistic. Instead of being programmed with rules, generative AI relies on examining and learning from large datasets to produce original outputs.

Some key characteristics of generative AI:

- Generates brand new content, rather than just classifying or labeling existing data. The outputs are not based on predefined templates or rules.
- Uses machine learning techniques like neural networks to train on large datasets, allowing the models to learn the patterns and relationships in data.
- Outputs are often probabilistic (i.e., most likely) and reflect the statistical relationships learned from the training data. This allows variation and diversity in the generated content.
- Generates artifacts that mimic styles, structures, and patterns seen in the training data. This allows high-quality, realistic outputs.

Some major types and examples of generative AI:

- **Generative adversarial networks (GANs):** GANs use two neural networks – one generates candidates while the other discriminates real from fake. This pushes the generator to create more realistic outputs. GANs have produced very convincing generated images and videos.
- **Variational autoencoders (VAEs):** VAEs are neural networks that compress data into a latent space and can generate new data having similar characteristics to the training data. VAEs are good for creating diverse outputs.
- **Diffusion models:** These generate data by starting with random noise and modifying it iteratively to introduce attributes of real data based on diffusion process modeling. DALL-E 2 uses a diffusion model to create novel images from text captions.
- **Reinforcement learning:** RL agents are rewarded for actions that maximize a goal. This allows generative models to create content aimed at specific objectives, like maximizing user engagement.
- **Transformers:** Transformer-based architectures like GPT excel at generating coherent, high-quality text by learning contextual relationships in language from large text corpora.

Generative AI has diverse applications across industries like generating code, chemical structures, art, 3D shapes, synthetic media, and more. It promises to revolutionize content creation and automation. But it also raises concerns about misuse of realistic generated content and data privacy. Nonetheless, generative AI represents an exciting new frontier in AI research and application. Let's look more closely at these five types.

Generative Adversarial Networks (GANs)

Generative adversarial networks (GANs) are a powerful type of generative model that uses two neural networks competing against each other to generate new, synthetic data that closely resembles real-world data.

The two neural networks are:

- **Generator:** This neural network generates new data instances (images, text, etc.) from random noise. It starts creating low-quality outputs but improves over time.
- **Discriminator:** This neural network receives data instances from both the generator and real-world training data, and tries to determine which are fake (from the generator) and which are real.

The two networks play a minimax adversarial game – the generator tries to fool the discriminator by creating increasingly realistic data, while the discriminator tries to correctly classify the real and fake data. This process of competition forces the generator to improve continuously until the generated outputs become indistinguishable from real data.

GANs can produce incredibly realistic generated photos of human faces, animals, objects, and scenes that are very difficult to differentiate from real images. By sampling different points in the latent noise space, GANs can also generate highly diverse and unique outputs.

GANs are also used to generate ultra-realistic profile pictures on social media, create fake celebrity footage in forged videos, synthesize speech in the voice of a person with just a few samples, and other such applications. However, the potential for misuse of such realistic forged content has raised both ethical and privacy concerns.

Overall, the minimax game and adversarial training make GANs very effective at mimicking intricate patterns in data distributions and producing new data points that plausibly belong to those distributions. This makes them a popular architecture for multiple generative modeling tasks.

Variational Autoencoders (VAEs)

Variational autoencoders (VAEs) are a type of generative model that use neural networks for compressing data into a lower-dimensional latent space and generating new data from sampling points in that space.

VAEs consist of:

- An encoder neural network that compresses input data into a compact latent representation or code.
- A decoder neural network that reconstructs the original input from the latent code.

During training, the VAE learns to optimize the encoder and decoder to allow converting data to and from the latent space, which captures the most salient features and variations in the data.

Once trained, the VAE allows:

- Encoding any data into the latent space and decoding it back, which serves as a means of compression and reconstruction.
- Generating entirely new data by sampling random points in the latent space and decoding them. The new samples retain similarities to the training data but represent novel variations.

Unlike GANs that require finding a fine balance during training, VAEs directly optimize for the ability to reconstruct data from the latent space, making them more stable to train. VAEs can generate diverse data by sampling in the latent space.

Applications of VAEs include:

- Creating new human faces, animals, objects, etc. with different variations.
- Generating molecular structures and chemical compounds with desired properties.
- Producing novel voices by conditioning the sampling on attributes like tone, accent, etc.
- Recommending product variations and designs based on initial concepts.

A major advantage of VAEs is the ability to intentionally guide the characteristics of generated data by manipulating the latent code vectors. Overall, VAEs offer a flexible framework for data-efficient generative modeling.

Diffusion Models

Diffusion models are a class of generative models that create realistic data by gradually modifying random noise through a diffusion process. The process has two main steps:

- Forward diffusion: The model starts with real training data and adds Gaussian noise to it iteratively resulting in detached noisy data. This destroys details while retaining high-level structure.
- Reverse diffusion: Starts with pure noise and performs iterative refinement while removing some noise at each step. This gradually enhances details and introduces attributes of real data.

Mathematically, diffusion models employ a Markov chain to model how noise evolves over time (diffuses) through the data. By learning to reverse this diffusion, the model can start from noise and generate data with realistic attributes.

A key advantage is that diffusion models can condition the reverse diffusion on context like class labels or captions to directly generate targeted outputs.

For example, DALL-E 2 uses a diffusion model conditioned on text captions to generate novel, high-quality images reflecting the caption meaning. It starts with random noise and slowly edits it over hundreds of steps while matching the evolving image to the caption at each point.

Other applications of diffusion models include creating synthetic voices, generating molecular structures with desired properties, producing realistic 3D shapes, and rendering novel scenes or human poses based on descriptions.

Overall, diffusion models allow fine-grained control over the incremental generation process to craft high-quality, targeted results. Their ability to condition on context makes them suited for controllable generation tasks compared to methods that directly output complete results.

Reinforcement Learning

Reinforcement learning (RL) is a technique that trains AI agents to take optimal actions in an environment to maximize cumulative rewards. This can be applied to train generative models as well.

In RL-based generative modeling:

- The generative model produces candidate artifacts like images, text, music, etc., based on current state.
- The artifacts are evaluated against a reward function designed to assess quality, novelty, diversity, and objectives like user engagement.
- The generator model is reinforced to produce outputs that can obtain higher rewards in the future.

Over successive iterations, the generator learns to create artifacts that score highly on the specified reward criteria.

For example, an RL-trained generative model can:

- Generate news headlines aimed at driving more user clicks by rewarding clickbait-sounding titles.
- Synthesize product images or music that are more likely to elicit positive responses from target users based on their preferences.
- Create levels in games that are engaging and challenging for players by using player metrics as rewards.

Unlike supervised learning which optimizes for resemblance to training data, RL directly optimizes for external goals specified via rewards. This makes RL suitable for generative modeling requiring purpose-driven, customized outputs.

However, designing the right rewards functions can be challenging. Bad rewards can lead to undesirable generated content. Overall though, RL provides a way to steer generative models towards practical objectives.

Transformers

Transformers are a class of neural network architecture that have driven major advances in generative modeling for text, becoming the dominant approach nowadays.

Transformers process input text by attending to context using a mechanism called self-attention. This allows modeling long-range dependencies in language better than recurrent neural networks.

Key advantages of transformers for generative text AI:

- Self-attention learns contextual relationships between words and sentences across large corpora. This allows generating text that is coherent, logical, and consistent.

- Stacking multiple self-attention layers allows modeling hierarchical structure and long-term coherence in generated text.
- Parallel processing of sequence positions increases speed and allows training on huge text corpora.
- Conditioning the text generation on past context (previous tokens) allows more relevant, targeted continuation of text.

GPT-4 is a massive auto-regressive transformer network trained on over 1 trillion parameters. It achieves state-of-the-art performance in generative language tasks like continuing prompts with logical, human-like text.

Other transformer-based models like CTRL, GROVER, TransfoXL and GPT-Neo also demonstrate strong performance on text generation benchmarks, showing the power of self-attention.

Limitations include large computational requirements for training and generation, and potential for generating toxic or biased text if the training data contains such attributes.

Overall, transformers allow modeling the real-world complexity and nuance of language more effectively compared to earlier methods. This makes them indispensable for AI assistants, chatbots, summarization, story generation, and other text-based generative applications.

Conclusion

In summary, generative AI refers to a cutting-edge class of artificial intelligence technologies that create novel, realistic artifacts like images, videos, text, 3D models, and more from scratch. Instead of following predefined rules, generative AI models develop creative capabilities by learning to represent and generate data that conforms to the patterns in their training datasets through techniques like neural networks and adversarial training.

Key generative AI methods highlighted in this chapter include generative adversarial networks, variational autoencoders, diffusion models, reinforcement learning agents, and transformer-based models. Each approach has its strengths and applications, from generating highly realistic synthetic media using GANs to creating coherent text using transformers like GPT.

The applications of generative AI span multiple industries and use cases, ranging from enhancing creativity for artists to automating repetitive tasks and augmenting human capabilities. However, concerns remain about potential misuse of forged media, biases perpetuated through data, and legal implications surrounding copyright and data rights. Huge amounts of research is focused on improving the capabilities, controllability, and social responsibility of generative AI systems.

Overall, generative AI represents an enormously promising field that is rapidly evolving and contributing towards more capable, autonomous AI systems. The next decade will likely see generative models become indispensable tools across many sectors and potentially even taking over creative jobs. Going forward, developing frameworks to ensure ethics, fairness, and transparency should be prioritized to fully realize the benefits of this transformative technology.

Unleashing Creativity: The Magic of Generative Pre-trained Transformers

In today's era of ever-advancing technology, we are witnessing remarkable breakthroughs in various fields. From healthcare to transportation, the realm of Artificial Intelligence (AI) has provided inventive solutions to numerous challenges. One such innovation that has revolutionized the world of natural language generation is Generative Pre-trained Transformers (GPT). In this chapter, we will delve into the fascinating world of GPT, exploring its inner workings, evolution, and the profound benefits it brings to society.

The Birth of GPT

The birth of Generative Pre-trained Transformers (GPT) can be accredited to OpenAI, a renowned research organization at the forefront of AI advancements. GPT emerged as an extension of the already groundbreaking Transformers model, which brought about a paradigm shift in the field of machine learning.

Transformers revolutionized natural language processing by introducing the attention mechanism. Traditional language models struggled with contextual understanding, often generating text that lacked coherence and fluency. The attention mechanism changed that by enabling the model to weigh and focus on relevant words or phrases in the input text, allowing for a more nuanced understanding of language.

Building upon the success of Transformers, OpenAI further refined the model with the introduction of GPT. GPT took the attention mechanism a step further by incorporating the concept of pre-training and fine-tuning, which elevated the model's generative capabilities.

Pre-training is the initial stage of training in GPT. During pre-training, the model is exposed to vast amounts of text data, such as books, research papers, posts, or internet sources. By training on this massive corpus of data, GPT learns grammar, factual knowledge, and commonsense reasoning. This process enables the model to develop a comprehensive understanding of language, capturing the intricate nuances and patterns that exist within it.

After pre-training, GPT enters the fine-tuning phase. In this stage, the model is trained on more specific tasks to adapt it for particular applications. For example, GPT can be fine-tuned for tasks like translation, summarization, or even creative writing. The fine-tuning process helps the model specialize its knowledge towards a specific domain, enabling it to generate highly relevant and accurate text within that context.

By combining the power of pre-training and fine-tuning, GPT becomes truly generative. It possesses a deep understanding of language and the capacity to generate coherent and contextually aware responses. This breakthrough in natural language generation has revolutionized various industries and applications, paving the way for enhanced content creation, translation services, virtual assistants, and more.

GPT has since undergone several iterations, with GPT-4 being the most recent and impressive release from OpenAI. GPT-4 showcases the astonishing capabilities of these generative language models, producing text that is virtually indistinguishable from something a human would write. It is a testament to the enormous potential of GPT models to understand and generate language with incredible fluency and creativity.

The birth of GPT, as indicated, can be traced back to the foundation laid by Transformers and the introduction of the attention mechanism. OpenAI's innovative implementation of pre-training and fine-tuning has taken this technology to new heights, enabling GPT to truly comprehend language and generate text that is valuable and coherent. The journey of GPT validates the power of continuous research and innovation – driving us toward a future where AI-assisted language generation becomes an essential tool in our daily lives.

Understanding GPT

To truly grasp the inner workings of Generative Pre-trained Transformers, it is beneficial to dive deeper into how GPT understands and generates language. GPT leverages large-scale unsupervised learning, which means it learns from vast amounts of data without explicit labels or guidance.

The pre-training phase lies at the core of GPT's language understanding capabilities. During pre-training, the model is exposed to a massive corpus of diverse textual data, which can include books, research papers, posts, websites, and more. The model meticulously analyzes this data, delving into its syntactic structures, grammar, factual knowledge, and contextual nuances. Through this process, GPT strives to develop a comprehensive understanding of language itself.

By training on such diverse and extensive data sources, GPT learns to recognize common patterns, grasp the meaning behind words, and infer relationships between them. This pre-training phase equips the model with the ability to generate coherent responses and make contextually appropriate choices.

After pre-training, GPT enters the fine-tuning phase. During fine-tuning, the model is trained on specific tasks or domains to specialize its language generation capabilities. For example, it can be fine-tuned for translating text between languages, summarizing documents, or even composing creative writing pieces. This process refines the model's understanding of the specific task at hand and optimizes its ability to generate high-quality and relevant responses within that domain.

As we mentioned, the underlying architecture of GPT relies on Transformers, which revolutionized natural language processing by introducing the attention mechanism. Transformers break down text into tokens, which are smaller units like words or subwords. GPT processes these tokens in parallel, allowing the model to capture and remember relationships between words more effectively.

The attention mechanism in GPT allows the model to weigh and focus on relevant parts of the input text. This mechanism is crucial for understanding and generating coherent responses. By giving attention to specific words or phrases that are most relevant to the context, GPT can generate highly contextual and fluent outputs.

Crucially, GPT's ability to process information in parallel and capture word dependencies allows it to generate text that is not only grammatically correct but also contextually meaningful and logical. This architectural design, coupled with the pre-training and fine-tuning process, equips GPT with the power to understand and generate language with impressive fluency and accuracy.

Overall, GPT leverages large-scale unsupervised learning through pre-training on vast amounts of textual data. Its understanding of language and contextual nuances is enhanced through this data-driven training. The subsequent fine-tuning phase optimizes GPT's language generation capabilities for specific tasks. Through the Transformer architecture and attention mechanisms, GPT processes words or subwords in parallel, capturing intricate relationships between them. These mechanisms enable GPT to generate text that is not only grammatically sound but also contextually meaningful and coherent.

Applications of GPT

The applications of GPT are seemingly limitless, with the technology finding its way into various industries. Here are a few ways GPT is enhancing business operations:

Content Creation

Content creation is a fundamental aspect of communication and marketing in today's digital age. Whether it's engaging emails, captivating social media captions, persuasive advertisements, or informative posts, the demand for high-quality content is ever-increasing. This is where Generative Pre-trained Transformers (GPT) shine, revolutionizing the way we generate written content.

Its remarkable ability to produce coherent and context-aware text has transformed the content creation landscape. Content creators and marketers now have a powerful tool at their disposal that can assist, inspire, and enhance their creative processes.

One of the key advantages of using GPT in content creation is its versatility. GPT can adapt to different writing styles, tones, and genres, allowing content creators to seamlessly produce material in a variety of formats. Whether it's catchy headlines, engaging product descriptions, or appealing storytelling, GPT can generate text that aligns with the desired tone and objective.

GPT's language generation capabilities can also significantly speed up the content creation process. It can assist writers by providing suggestions, helping them overcome writer's block, and offering alternative phrasing options. Instead of starting from scratch, content creators can begin with a generated prompt and refine it to match their specific requirements. This collaboration between humans and AI creates a symbiotic relationship, allowing content creators to leverage the unique strengths of GPT to enhance their creativity.

For marketers, GPT is a valuable resource in developing persuasive and impactful advertising copy. Whether it's crafting compelling email subject lines, optimizing website landing pages, or creating engaging social media posts, GPT's ability to understand context and generate relevant text is a game-changer. By leveraging GPT, marketers can tap into its creativity and linguistic prowess to produce persuasive messages that resonate with their target audience.

Moreover, GPT can assist businesses in generating content at scale. When faced with the challenge of creating a large volume of content, GPT can generate initial drafts or even complete sections, minimizing the time and effort required. This enables companies to streamline their content creation processes, freeing up resources to focus on other strategic initiatives.

However, it's important to note that while GPT is a powerful tool, human input and review remain crucial. Content creators must ensure that the generated text aligns with their brand voice, adheres to ethical guidelines, and maintains accuracy and factual correctness. Responsible use of this technology produces the best outcomes.

GPT's impact on content creation cannot be overstated. From providing inspiration and overcoming writer's block to generating entire pieces of content, GPT empowers content creators and marketers to produce high-quality, contextually relevant, and engaging content. By collaborating with this innovative technology, content creators can unlock new levels of creativity and efficiency that will shape the future of content creation. In this way, the partnership between human creativity and AI assistance has the potential to revolutionize the way we communicate and engage with audiences across various platforms.

Language Translation

Language translation is a vital aspect of global communication, facilitating understanding and connectivity between people from diverse linguistic backgrounds. The advent of Generative Pre-trained Transformers (GPT) has significantly advanced the field of machine translation, revolutionizing the way we overcome language barriers.

GPT's ability to understand and generate text in multiple languages has opened up new horizons for language translation services. Traditionally, machine translation systems struggled with accurately capturing the nuances, idioms, and cultural context of different languages. However, GPT's fine-tuning capabilities have pushed out the boundaries of accuracy and fluency in translation, resulting in more refined, human-like translations.

Fine-tuning GPT for language translation involves training the model on bilingual or multilingual datasets. This process allows the model to comprehend the syntactic and semantic structures of different languages, their word alignments, and even cultural nuances. Through exposure to an extensive range of translated texts, GPT becomes proficient in transforming text from one language to another while maintaining the integrity of the original message.

GPT's multi-lingual translation abilities benefit individuals, businesses, and organizations across various sectors. For example, in individual use, GPT-powered translation services enable seamless communication while traveling, working, or connecting with people from different linguistic backgrounds. It helps break down language barriers, fostering inclusivity and global collaboration.

In the business world, however, accurate translation is crucial for effective communication with international clients, partners, and customers. GPT-powered translation systems provide businesses with the ability to localize their content, ensuring that their messages are conveyed accurately and appropriately within different cultural contexts. This opens up new markets and opportunities for global expansion.

Furthermore, GPT's translation capabilities have found applications in the e-commerce industry. With the rise of global online marketplaces, accurate and real-time translation of product descriptions, customer reviews, and user-generated content is essential for creating a seamless customer experience. GPT can help automate the translation process, enabling businesses to efficiently reach a global customer base.

In the field of education, GPT-supported translation services enable students and researchers to access and comprehend academic resources and research papers written in different languages. This promotes knowledge sharing and collaboration across borders, transcending language barriers for the betterment of academia and innovation.

It is important to note that GPT-powered translation systems are not meant to replace human translators. Human expertise and cultural sensitivity remain invaluable in achieving culturally appropriate and highly nuanced translations. However, GPT provides a significant boost to the translation process, allowing for increased efficiency, scalability, and accessibility.

In the field of language translation, GPT's fine-tuning capabilities have propelled machine translation to new heights, improving both accuracy and fluency.. This breakthrough technology enhances communication and connectivity across language barriers and fosters global understanding. From enabling seamless travel experiences to streamlining international business operations, GPT's language translation capabilities have a profound impact on society and pave the way for a more connected and inclusive world.

Virtual Assistants and Chatbots

Virtual assistants and chatbots have become increasingly commonplace in our daily lives. These AI-powered conversation agents have transformed how we engage with technology and access information. At the core of these sophisticated conversational AI systems lies Generative Pre-trained Transformers (GPT), which enables them to understand natural language inputs and generate human-like responses.

GPT's language understanding capabilities are a game-changer for virtual assistants and chatbots. These systems can decode and comprehend the intricacies of natural language, gaining an understanding of the intent, context, and nuances within a user's query. This allows them to provide relevant and accurate responses, enhancing the user experience (UX) and enabling more efficient interactions between humans and machines.

The power of GPT in this arena lies in its ability to process and analyze large volumes of text data during pre-training. By training on diverse data sources, GPT learns patterns, grammatical structures, and contextual cues that form the foundation of human language. It's this deep understanding that allows virtual assistants and chatbots to interpret and comprehend the intent behind user queries, even when they are phrased conversationally or with variations in vocabulary.

GPT's generative capabilities then enable virtual assistants and chatbots to generate responses that emulate human-like conversation based on the input they receive. By considering the context and user intent, GPT-powered chatbots tailor their answers to provide relevant information and assist users effectively.

There is a wide variety of applications for these AI-powered conversational systems powered by GPT. Virtual assistants like Amazon's Alexa, Google Assistant, Apple's Siri, and Microsoft's Cortana are now integral parts of our lives; they help us with tasks such as setting reminders, providing weather updates, answering general knowledge questions, and even playing music. Their ability to understand and generate human-like responses creates a more natural and seamless interaction, enhancing their overall utility and acceptability.

Moreover, chatbots, deployed in various industries, offer personalized assistance, handle routine inquiries, and augment customer service. As chatbots continue to evolve, GPT's contributions enable them to handle complex queries, troubleshoot technical issues, and guide users through various processes. Whether it's a customer support chatbot on an e-commerce website, a healthcare chatbot providing initial diagnosis, or a banking chatbot assisting with financial transactions, GPT plays a crucial role in enhancing the effectiveness and efficiency of these interactions.

However, GPT-powered virtual assistants and chatbots not only benefit users by providing quick and accurate assistance but also bring numerous advantages to businesses. By leveraging conversational AI systems, businesses can offer round-the-clock support, handle large volumes of inquiries simultaneously, and maintain consistency in customer interactions. This translates to improved customer satisfaction, increased efficiency, and cost-saving benefits.

While GPT has greatly enhanced virtual assistants and chatbots, it's crucial to keep ethical considerations in mind. Responsible usage of AI systems is paramount to ensure accurate and unbiased information provision, protect privacy, and maintain appropriate boundaries of conversational exchanges.

Nevertheless, GPT's language understanding and generative capabilities have revolutionized the field of conversational AI systems. Virtual assistants and chatbots, powered by GPT, provide natural and contextually relevant interactions, improving user experiences and enhancing customer support services across various industries. As this technology continues to advance, we can expect even more sophisticated and human-like conversations with AI-powered virtual assistants and chatbots, enabling us to seamlessly interact with technology for our day-to-day needs.

Automating Customer Support

Customer support plays a vital role in ensuring customer satisfaction and maintaining positive relationships between businesses and their clients. However, the increasing volume of customer inquiries can place a significant burden on support teams, resulting in long wait times and potential service gaps. This is where GPT-powered chatbots and virtual assistants come in, revolutionizing the customer support landscape by automating routine inquiries and providing personalized assistance.

GPT-powered systems excel in handling routine inquiries and frequently asked questions, allowing customers to quickly find answers to common queries without requiring human intervention. Through their language understanding capabilities, these systems can comprehend the context and intent behind customer inquiries, providing accurate and relevant responses. Whether it's inquiries about product availability, shipping information, or account-related questions, GPT-powered chatbots are capable of efficiently handling all routine tasks.

Personalization is a key component of exceptional customer support, and GPT-powered systems can offer tailored assistance. By leveraging data from customer profiles and past interactions, these systems can provide personalized recommendations, troubleshoot common issues, and even offer targeted product suggestions based on individual preferences and purchase history. This level of personalized assistance enhances the customer experience, making customers feel valued and understood.

Moreover, GPT-powered systems can provide product information and support by understanding and interpreting complex requests. These systems have been trained on vast amounts of data, which allows them to possess extensive knowledge about a wide range of products and services. They can guide customers through product features, specifications, and usage instructions, ensuring a seamless and informed customer experience.

By automating routine inquiries and providing personalized assistance, GPT-powered chatbots and virtual assistants significantly reduce the workload on human customer support agents. This frees up valuable resources, allowing human agents to focus on more complex customer issues that require critical thinking, problem-solving, sensitive judgement calls, and empathy. Ultimately, the collaboration between GPT-powered systems and human support teams leads to more efficient customer support processes and improved customer satisfaction.

Implementing GPT-powered customer support systems also provides scalability for businesses. As customer inquiries increase, these systems can handle a larger volume of requests simultaneously without experiencing fatigue or diminishing performance. Moreover, these AI-powered systems ensure consistency in response quality, reducing the risk of human error or bias.

However, it is important to strike a balance between automation and human interaction. While GPT-powered systems are capable and efficient in handling routine inquiries, there may be instances where complex or sensitive customer issues require the empathetic touch of a human agent. Combining the power of GPT with human expertise allows businesses to provide comprehensive support that meets the diverse needs of their customers.

Overall, GPT-powered chatbots and virtual assistants have revolutionized customer support by automating routine inquiries, offering personalized assistance, and providing product information. By leveraging their language understanding capabilities, these systems not only enhance customer experience but free up human resources and provide scalable support. As businesses embrace the potential of GPT in customer support operations, they can improve service efficiency, increase customer satisfaction, and build stronger relationships with their clientele.

The Ethical Considerations

As Generative Pre-trained Transformers (GPT) technology continues to evolve and gain widespread adoption, it is essential to address the ethical considerations that arise. While GPT offers significant benefits to society, there is a responsibility to mitigate potential risks and ensure its ethical and responsible usage.

One prevalent concern is the potential for misuse in generating fake news posts, spreading misinformation, or generating malicious content. GPT's capacity to generate human-like text raises the possibility of creating deceptive content that can mislead and harm individuals or communities. This poses a threat to public trust, democratic processes, and societal well-being.

To address these concerns, responsible users of GPT must prioritize the development and implementation of robust safeguards. These safeguards can include measures such as content moderation, fact-checking, and filtering mechanisms to ensure that the generated content is accurate, unbiased, and aligned with ethical standards. Collaboration between technology developers, policymakers, and the wider community is essential in shaping guidelines and regulations that govern the responsible use of GPT.

Transparency is another crucial ethical consideration. Users of GPT should be aware that they are interacting with an AI system and not a human. Maintaining transparency helps to manage user expectations, prevent potential harm, and ensure the responsible deployment of GPT-powered applications. Companies developing GPT-powered systems must make efforts to clearly disclose the nature of the interaction and provide insights into the capabilities and limitations of the technology.

Guarding user privacy and data protection is paramount. GPT-powered systems may process and store user data to improve performance and personalize the user experience. To uphold ethical standards, it is essential to not only obtain user consent but also ensure data security and adhere to relevant privacy regulations. Strict data protection measures should be in place to prevent unauthorized access, breaches, or misuse of user information.

Bias and discrimination are additional concerns when it comes to AI applications, including GPT. We'll discuss bias in more detail in the section on Prompt Engineering. But the data used for pre-training and fine-tuning can inadvertently embed biases present in the training data, leading to biased or discriminatory outputs. Addressing these biases requires a proactive approach, including diverse and representative training data, thorough evaluation of system outputs, and continuous monitoring and adjustment of models to minimize bias and ensure fairness.

As GPT continues to advance, responsible development and deployment must prioritize the avoidance of harm. Ethical considerations should be integrated into the entire lifecycle of GPT-powered systems, from data collection and model design to system implementation and ongoing monitoring. Regular audits and assessments should be conducted to identify potential risks and ensure adherence to ethical guidelines.

Both public engagement and transparency play a crucial role in addressing ethical considerations related to GPT. Collaboration with stakeholders, including experts, policymakers, and end-users, promotes open discussions, knowledge sharing, and the development of consensus around ethical guidelines. This collective effort will enable the responsible and beneficial use of GPT technology while navigating potential challenges and risks.

It has become clear over time that while the potential of GPT technology is vast and transformative, it is accompanied by significant ethical considerations. Responsible development, robust safeguards, transparency, privacy protection, bias mitigation, and public engagement are vital components in harnessing the true potential of GPT – while ensuring its usage aligns with societal values, promotes trust, and avoids misuse. By adhering to ethical principles, GPT can continue to drive positive impact and offer valuable benefits to society.

The Future of GPT

The future of GPT holds unprecedented potential for advancements in natural language generation, pushing out the boundaries of what is possible in the realm of AI-powered language models. OpenAI's release of GPT-4 signifies the continued progress in this field, with the model exhibiting astonishing capabilities that blur the lines between machine-generated and human-written text.

GPT-4 showcases significantly improved fluency, coherence, and contextuality over previous iterations when generating text. It can produce responses that are almost indistinguishable from those written by humans, making interactions with AI-powered language models more seamless and natural than ever. The advancements in GPT-4 and future iterations therefore have vast implications for various fields and applications.

Education is one area where GPT's future holds promise. In the classroom, GPT-powered systems can provide personalized tutoring, answer students' questions, and assist with assignments. By engaging with GPT, students may experience interactive learning experiences that adapt to their individual needs, fostering enhanced engagement and comprehension. GPT can also assist educators in developing high-quality educational content and resources, revolutionizing the way knowledge is disseminated.

Creative writing is another domain where GPT's future shines brightly. Creative writers can collaborate with GPT to generate story ideas, co-author works, or receive inspiration and suggestions for enhancing their writing. GPT's deep understanding of language and context allows it to contribute unique perspectives and generate creative text that complements human creativity. This collaboration between human and AI creativity can foster a new era of storytelling and artistic expression.

Accessibility is another critical area where GPT can have a transformative impact. By leveraging GPT technology, individuals with disabilities, such as those with speech or motor impairments, can communicate more effectively. GPT-powered assistive technology can facilitate text-to-speech conversion, help generate written content, and enable inclusive communication across various platforms. These advancements empower individuals to participate fully in society and express themselves in ways they might not have previously imagined.

However – and we emphasize this again – while GPT's future is promising, it will still be essential to address any ethical concerns that may arise. Ensuring transparency, accountability, and responsible usage will be key as language models become more sophisticated. Ongoing research and collaboration between researchers, developers, policymakers, and the wider community are crucial in defining ethical guidelines, addressing potential biases, and ensuring that GPT is leveraged for the collective benefit of society.

Additionally, as GPT models continue to evolve, considerations must also be given to energy efficiency and sustainability. Training and running large language models like GPT-4 can require significant computational resources, which may have environmental implications. Exploring strategies such as model optimization and efficient training techniques is critical for minimizing energy consumption and the carbon footprint associated with these models.

Overall, the future of GPT holds immense potential for transformative advancements in natural language generation. GPT-4's ability to generate human-like text marks a significant milestone, offering remarkable possibilities in education, creative writing, accessibility, and beyond. Responsible deployment, continued research, and ethical considerations will play critical roles in harnessing this potential to create a future where AI-powered language models like GPT contribute positively to our lives, enabling us to communicate, learn, and create in ways that were once unimaginable.

Conclusion

In conclusion, Generative Pre-trained Transformers (GPT) have revolutionized the landscape of natural language generation. From content creation to language translation, virtual assistants, chatbots, and beyond, GPT's transformative abilities have reshaped various industries and enriched society as a whole. By leveraging this technology responsibly and ethically, we can tap into the vast potential of GPT to unlock a future filled with unprecedented opportunities.

However, as we witness the tremendous advantages that GPT offers, it is imperative to approach its implementation with careful consideration of ethical guidelines and responsible usage. By doing so, we can harness the power of GPT to enhance our communication, streamline processes, and foster creativity while ensuring that its deployment aligns with our values and safeguards the well-being of individuals and communities.

Language Models: From RNNs to Transformers

Artificial intelligence has witnessed remarkable advancements in the field of natural language processing, leading to the rise of technologies such as large language models and Generative Pre-trained Transformers (GPT). These innovations have revolutionized various applications, ranging from chatbots to content generation. In this chapter, we will delve into the key differences and similarities between these powerful AI technologies, shedding light on their unique capabilities and the implications they carry.

Understanding Large Language Models

Traditional large language models, such as GPT-4 by OpenAI, utilize a sequential approach to generate text. These models rely on recurrent neural networks (RNNs) or long short-term memory (LSTM) networks to process natural language.

GPT-4, like its predecessors, inherits the autoregressive nature of traditional language models. It predicts the next word in a sentence by considering the context of the previous words and leveraging the patterns, grammar, and context inherent to natural language. By generating text one word at a time, these models aim to produce coherent and human-like sentences.

However, the sequential generation process in models like GPT-4 comes with certain limitations. One of the major challenges lies in the lack of efficient parallelization. Since each word's prediction is dependent on the preceding context, it becomes difficult to parallelize the computation across multiple processing units. Consequently, when processing large volumes of text, these models can be computationally demanding and relatively slow.

Another limitation is the sensitivity to long-range dependencies. As the length of the text increases, traditional language models struggle to retain information from earlier parts of the sentence, leading to a potential loss of context and coherence in longer passages.

To overcome these limitations, the evolution of language models has incorporated the power of Transformers. Transformers, with their attention mechanisms and parallelizable architecture, offer a more effective solution for language understanding and generation.

GPT-4 implements the Transformer architecture to enable more efficient parallelization and better capture long-range dependencies in text.

By adopting Transformers, GPT-4 is equipped to process and generate text in parallel, significantly improving computational efficiency. Furthermore, the elaborate attention mechanisms within Transformers empower GPT-4 to understand contextual relationships between words across longer sequences, ensuring better coherence and maintaining the overall context of the generated text.

As GPT-4 builds upon the success of its predecessors, it holds the potential to be a significant leap forward in producing high-quality, contextually-rich text generation.

Introducing Generative Pre-trained Transformers (GPT)

Generative Pre-trained Transformers (GPT) technology takes language models to the next level. Developed by OpenAI, GPT utilizes the Transformer architecture, a neural network designed to capture relationships between different words in a more efficient and parallelizable way than traditional language models.

Unlike autoregressive models, GPT is trained using a "pre-training and fine-tuning" approach. During the pre-training stage, the model is fed with a large corpus of unlabeled text, such as books or internet posts, and learns to predict the missing words within sentences. This process equips the model with a deep understanding of language and a rich representation of textual information.

Once pre-training is complete, GPT is fine-tuned on specific tasks by exposing it to labeled data for tasks like text completion, translation, or sentiment analysis. By capitalizing on the pre-trained knowledge, GPT demonstrates superior performance across a wide range of natural language processing tasks.

Unleashing the Power of Transformers:

The introduction of the Transformer architecture was a game-changer in the field of natural language processing. Its key components, such as self-attention mechanisms and multi-head attention, allow for parallelization and capture long-range dependencies in text efficiently.

The self-attention mechanism calculates the importance of each word in the context of the entire sentence, enabling the model to incorporate relevant information from any position. The multi-head attention mechanism allows the model to focus on different parts of the input simultaneously, facilitating a more comprehensive understanding of the text's structure.

Differences between Large Language Models and GPT

Architecture

One key difference between large language models and GPT lies in their underlying architecture. While traditional large language models rely on recurrent neural networks (RNNs) or long short-term memory (LSTM) networks, GPT utilizes the Transformer architecture. Transformers are based on a self-attention mechanism that allows for parallelizable computation, making GPT more efficient in processing text compared to the sequential processing of RNN-based models.

The parallelizable nature of Transformers enables GPT to process multiple words simultaneously, resulting in faster and more efficient text generation. This architectural distinction gives GPT an advantage in processing large volumes of text, as it can harness the power of parallel processing units.

Pre-training Approach

Another notable difference lies in the pre-training approach used by traditional large language models and GPT. Traditional models typically undergo autoregressive training, where they predict one word at a time based on the previous context. In contrast, GPT incorporates a pre-training and fine-tuning approach.

During the pre-training phase, GPT is exposed to unlabeled text from a large corpus, learning to predict missing words within sentences. This process provides the model with a strong understanding of language and a rich representation of textual information. In the subsequent fine-tuning stage, GPT is trained on specific tasks using labeled data.

This two-step approach gives GPT a head start as it has already captured a deep understanding of language during pre-training, enabling it to fine-tune on specific tasks more effectively. In contrast, traditional language models start from scratch without the benefit of a pre-trained knowledge base.

Contextual Understanding

GPT's utilization of the Transformer architecture enhances its ability to model long-range dependencies through self-attention mechanisms. This enables GPT to capture contextual relationships between words more effectively than traditional large language models.

By incorporating self-attention, GPT can assign varying levels of importance to different words in a sentence, considering the relationships between all words simultaneously. This contextual understanding allows GPT to generate text that maintains coherence and continuity.

Performance

GPT has demonstrated superior performance across a wide range of natural language processing tasks. The combination of the advanced Transformer architecture and the extensive pre-training GPT undergoes contributes to its remarkable performance.

GPT's architecture allows for more efficient parallel processing, enabling faster and more accurate text generation. The pre-training phase equips GPT with a comprehensive knowledge of language, improving its ability to generate contextually relevant and coherent responses.

Additionally, GPT's remarkable performance in natural language processing tasks, including language translation, text completion, and sentiment analysis, showcases its versatility and effectiveness as a language model.

While traditional large language models and GPT share the goal of text generation, they differ in architecture, pre-training approaches, contextual understanding, and performance. GPT's adoption of the Transformer architecture and pre-training/fine-tuning technique has proven to be a game-changer, exhibiting superior capabilities and performance in natural language processing tasks.

Similarities between Large Language Models and GPT

Language Generation

Both large language models and GPT share a common primary objective: generating human-like text. Whether it's producing responses in a chatbot or creating coherent paragraphs in a chapter, both models aim to generate text that resembles human language. They achieve this by learning patterns, grammar, context, and other linguistic nuances through extensive training on large datasets.

Training on Large Datasets

Both large language models and GPT require substantial amounts of data to train effectively. These models rely on vast corpora of text, often comprised of millions or even billions of words, to capture the intricacies of human language. By exposing these models to an extensive range of linguistic examples, they learn the statistical patterns and relationships necessary for generating coherent and contextually relevant text.

The training process involves iteratively fine-tuning the model's parameters to minimize errors and maximize its ability to generate high-quality text. Both kinds of models benefit from access to diverse and representative datasets, helping them learn a rich representation of language.

Fine-tuning

While the approaches differ, both large language models and GPT can be fine-tuned on specific tasks to enhance their performance and adapt to specific applications. Fine-tuning involves retraining the model on a more specific dataset related to the desired task or domain.

By fine-tuning, developers can customize the models to suit their specific needs, improving their output's accuracy and relevance in specialized contexts. This adaptability allows large language models and GPT to be flexible and versatile tools for various natural language processing tasks, including sentiment analysis, language translation, text summarization, and more.

Fine-tuning also plays a crucial role in addressing any limitations or biases that may arise during pre-training. It allows developers to refine the models' responses, ensuring they align with specific guidelines, ethical considerations, or domain-specific requirements.

In summary, despite their differences, large language models and GPT share important similarities. They both prioritize language generation, rely on large training datasets, and benefit from fine-tuning to optimize their performance for specific tasks. By building on these commonalities and leveraging their unique features, these models continue to advance the capabilities of AI-driven natural language processing, shaping the future of text generation.

Conclusion

In the realm of natural language processing, both large language models and Generative Pre-trained Transformers (GPT) have made significant strides in text generation. While they share the common goal of producing human-like text, GPT's incorporation of the powerful Transformer architecture sets it apart, enabling enhanced language understanding and generation capabilities.

GPT's utilization of the Transformer architecture allows for more efficient processing by leveraging parallelization and capturing long-range dependencies in text more effectively. This architecture overcomes the limitations of traditional large language models, which rely on sequential processing using recurrent neural networks or LSTM networks. GPT's ability to process information in parallel results in faster and more efficient text generation, particularly when handling large volumes of text.

Moreover, GPT's pre-training and fine-tuning approach genuinely differentiates it from traditional language models. Through pre-training, GPT develops a deep understanding of language by learning to predict missing words in unlabeled text. This rich pre-trained knowledge allows for more effective fine-tuning on specific tasks, improving its performance across a range of natural language processing applications.

The contextual understanding offered by GPT, thanks to the self-attention mechanisms of the Transformer architecture, further enhances its text generation capabilities. GPT can capture long-range dependencies, assign varying importance to words, and generate more coherent and informed responses.

In real-world outcomes, the deployment of GPT has demonstrated remarkable performance in various natural language processing tasks, surpassing traditional language models. The combination of the advanced architecture, pre-training, and fine-tuning provides GPT with a substantial advantage, making it a powerful tool for language generation.

Looking ahead, the future of AI-driven natural language processing holds promising developments. Researchers and developers continue to push the boundaries, exploring new horizons and finding innovative ways to enhance text generation and interaction. As these technologies evolve, we can expect more human-like AI systems and interactions that blur the lines between human-generated and AI-generated content.

Overall, large language models and Generative Pre-trained Transformers like ChatGPT have revolutionized natural language processing. While large language models paved the way, GPT's adoption of the Transformer architecture, pre-training approach, and contextual understanding have elevated the capabilities of AI-driven text generation. As we enter an era of increasingly sophisticated AI systems, the future holds exciting possibilities that will shape the way we interact with, rely on, and benefit from AI-generated content.

Harnessing Large Language Models for Strategic Decision-Making

In today's rapidly evolving business landscape, decision-making and strategic planning are critical elements for success. As a CEO, your ability to navigate complex challenges and capitalize on opportunities can be greatly enhanced by using advanced technologies. One such technology that has gained significant traction is the large language model, which combines language understanding with logical reasoning to provide sophisticated problem-solving and planning capabilities. In this chapter, we will explore how large language models can revolutionize your decision-making process and drive your organization towards unprecedented success.

Understanding Reasoning and Planning

Before we explore how large language models enable reasoning and planning, let's delve deeper into these concepts.

Reasoning

Reasoning involves the cognitive process of using existing knowledge, logic, and inference to arrive at conclusions or make decisions. It is the ability to connect facts, principles, and experiences to draw logical inferences and make informed judgments. Reasoning is driven by a combination of deductive (general to specific) and inductive (specific to general) thinking.

In the context of large language models, reasoning becomes an integral part of their decision-making process. These models possess vast knowledge acquired through pre-training on extensive textual data. When presented with a problem or a question, the model utilizes its understanding of language, along with logical inference, to arrive at a reasoned response. It looks for patterns, associations, and dependencies within the data it has learned from, enabling it to make well-informed decisions.

Planning

Planning involves creating strategies and processes to achieve specific goals. It requires a systematic approach to determine the sequence of steps necessary to accomplish a desired outcome. Planning encompasses defining objectives, evaluating options, considering constraints, and allocating resources efficiently.

In the context of large language models, planning complements reasoning by providing a structured framework for decision-making. These models possess the ability to generate meaningful and coherent sequences of actions based on their understanding of language and logical analysis. By incorporating reasoning into the planning process, the models can propose optimal courses of action to achieve a given goal or solve a problem.

How Large Language Models Enable Reasoning and Planning

Large language models, such as GPT are designed to process and understand vast amounts of textual information. Through pre-training on diverse text sources, these models learn patterns, relationships, and nuances in language use. This training equips the models with an extensive knowledge base, which they leverage during reasoning and planning tasks.

When presented with a query or problem, a large language model applies its language understanding capabilities to interpret the context and extract relevant information. It then uses logical inference to analyze the connections between different elements and generate potential solutions or action sequences. The model evaluates the implications, consequences, and feasibility of each step, considering various factors, constraints, and goals.

By combining reasoning and planning, large language models can propose well-thought-out strategies, foresee potential obstacles, and recommend novel approaches. These models can handle complex decision-making scenarios that involve multiple variables and uncertainties, providing valuable insights and support to CEOs in their strategic endeavors.

Reasoning and planning form two fundamental pillars of decision-making. Large language models leverage their language understanding capabilities and logical inference to excel in these areas. By comprehending linguistic nuances, analyzing patterns, and proposing coherent action sequences, these models empower CEOs with enhanced problem-solving abilities and informed decision-making. Understanding and utilizing the reasoning and planning capabilities of large language models can therefore unlock a world of opportunities, enabling businesses to thrive in an increasingly competitive and dynamic landscape.

Language Understanding and Inference

Large language models like GPT have undergone extensive pre-training on massive amounts of text data from diverse sources, as we mentioned earlier, enabling them to develop a comprehensive understanding of language. This pre-training process exposes the model to a wide range of linguistic patterns, contextual cues, and semantic relationships. As a result, these models acquire an inherent understanding of grammar, syntax, and semantics, allowing them to generate highly relevant and orderly responses.

What distinguishes large language models like GPT is their capacity to surpass simple response generation and venture into the realm of logic and reasoning. These models leverage their language understanding capabilities to not only provide accurate and contextually appropriate answers but also to infer and plan sequences of actions based on the given input.

By analyzing the context and comprehending the nuances of the text, language models can extract key information, identify patterns, and draw logical connections between different elements. This process of inference involves reasoning using the acquired knowledge to make informed decisions and generate meaningful output. In essence, language models can infer information that is not explicitly stated in the input but can be logically deduced from the available data.

For example, if presented with a question like "What steps should we take to improve customer satisfaction?", the language model can rely on its language understanding and inference capabilities to assess the context, evaluate different strategies, and generate a sequence of actions that may include enhancing customer support, improving product quality, and implementing personalized marketing campaigns. GPT can not only provide a list of potential actions but also prioritize and order them based on their relevance and feasibility.

This ability to reason and plan sets large language models apart from traditional rule-based systems or keyword-driven approaches. Instead of relying on a fixed set of rules or explicit instructions, these models leverage the inherent knowledge acquired during pre-training and dynamically generate responses and plans based on the input and the context in which it is presented.

This combination of language understanding and inference allows large language models to exhibit more sophisticated behavior and problem-solving abilities when compared to earlier AI approaches. CEOs can leverage these capabilities to gain deeper insights, obtain creative solutions, and make well-informed decisions in complex and ambiguous scenarios.

Large language models like GPT are not only skilled at comprehending language but also possess the unique ability to employ logic and reasoning to infer and plan sequences of actions. This makes them powerful tools for CEOs – enabling them to navigate challenges, seize opportunities, and make strategic decisions with enhanced accuracy and efficiency. Harnessing the potential of large language models in reasoning and planning can therefore significantly transform decision-making processes and drive organizations towards greater success and innovation.

Reasoning with Language Models

Language models like GPT possess remarkable reasoning abilities, which enable them to tackle complex queries and problems. By amalgamating their language understanding capabilities with the logical inference we mentioned above, these models generate a wide array of potential solutions or actions to address the given input. Let's dive deeper into how these models reason through language understanding and logical inference.

Language Understanding and Contextual Analysis

Large language models like GPT excel at language understanding, which involves comprehending the nuances and intricacies of the input text. Through extensive pre-training on massive amounts of data, these models learn to recognize and interpret the various components of language, including grammar, semantics, and syntax. This enables the model to grasp the context of the query or problem statement.

After analyzing the context of the input, language models can draw correlations, identify relevant information, and discern patterns within the text. They can recognize key entities, relationships, and dependencies, which are crucial for reasoning through the given information. This contextual analysis allows the model to form a foundational understanding upon which it can base its logical inferences.

Logical Inference and Knowledge Integration

Once the language model has a contextual understanding, it proceeds to engage in logical inference, combining its learned knowledge with the input data to generate potential solutions or actions. The model leverages the wealth of information it has been trained on to draw logical connections and make inferences about what the optimal next steps might be.

Based on the patterns, relationships, and dependencies identified within the context, the language model applies logical reasoning to propose potential solutions or action sequences. This involves weighing various factors, considering constraints, and evaluating the implications of each potential step. The model can generate new insights by recognizing similar patterns from its training data and adapting them to formulate novel solutions or sequences of actions.

It is important to note that these large language models employ statistical inference rather than strict deductive reasoning. They utilize the statistical patterns they have learned from training data to make probabilistic assessments and generate likely responses or action plans. The outputs provided by the model are based on the likelihood and statistical associations between the input and the learned data.

Iterative Reasoning and Improved Performance

Language models have significantly improved over the years, namely through advancements in architecture and training procedures. Techniques such as Transformers and pre-training with large-scale datasets have enabled models like GPT to reason more accurately and account for a wider range of contexts.

Moreover, training the models on a diverse array of data sources allows them to capture a broad spectrum of information, which enhances their reasoning capabilities. Exposing the models to a wide variety of texts means they can acquire knowledge from different domains and contexts, enabling them to reason across a broader range of topics.

Language models like GPT excel at reasoning by employing a combination of language understanding and logical inference. By analyzing the context, recognizing patterns, and drawing logical connections, these models generate potential solutions or action sequences. However, while their reasoning is based on statistical patterns and associations, these models have demonstrated remarkable problem-solving capabilities and have proven to be valuable decision-making tools.

By leveraging the reasoning abilities of language models, CEOs can tap into their expertise and make well-informed decisions. These models can provide insights, generate creative solutions, and propose action plans based on thorough contextual analysis and logical inference. Incorporating large language models into decision-making processes therefore empowers CEOs with enhanced problem-solving capabilities, ultimately driving their organizations towards success and innovation.

Planning Abilities of Language Models

One of the key strengths of large language models like GPT lies in their planning abilities. These models can go beyond mere understanding of the context and generate coherent and meaningful sequences of actions, providing valuable guidance in decision-making processes. Let's explore how their planning capabilities can be harnessed in complex scenarios.

Contextual Analysis and Goal Identification

Language models begin the planning process by analyzing the context, which includes understanding the given problem, identifying the desired outcome, and recognizing any constraints or limitations. By comprehending these elements, the model can set the foundation for generating a step-by-step plan of action.

The language model leverages its language understanding abilities to contextualize the problem and interpret the goals of the plan. This involves recognizing key entities, evaluating dependencies, and understanding the relationships between different elements in the input. By accurately capturing these nuances, the model ensures that the generated plan aligns with the desired outcome.

Sequencing Actions and Optimizing Solutions

Once the language model has a clear understanding of the context and goals, it employs its planning capabilities to propose a sequence of actions that lead to the desired outcome. The model generates a series of steps and organizes them in a logical and coherent manner, considering dependencies and prerequisites between actions.

During the planning process, the language model also takes into account any constraints or limitations that should be considered. It evaluates the feasibility and practicality of each action based on available resources, time constraints, and other relevant factors. This allows the model to optimize the plan by considering the most effective and efficient sequence of actions.

Considering Multiple Factors and Trade-offs

In complex decision-making scenarios, there are often multiple factors and trade-offs to consider. Language models excel at taking into account these complexities and proposing balanced plans that address various considerations. They can weigh different options, analyze potential risks and benefits, and even provide alternative solutions with varying trade-offs.

The ability of language models to integrate these diverse considerations into the planning process can be particularly valuable for CEOs. It enables them to evaluate different strategies, assess the potential impacts of each action, and make informed decisions based on a comprehensive analysis.

Value in Complex Decision-Making

The planning abilities of language models are particularly valuable in scenarios where complex decision-making is required. These models can handle intricate situations that involve multiple variables, dependencies, and uncertainties. Leveraging the vast knowledge acquired during pre-training, they can propose plans that account for various possibilities and adjust strategies in response to changing circumstances.

In addition, language models can quickly generate and iterate on plans, making them efficient tools for exploring different scenarios and considering alternative courses of action. This agility enables CEOs to proactively address challenges, evaluate potential outcomes, and make well-informed decisions.

It is important to note that, while language models offer valuable planning capabilities, the output should be carefully assessed and fine-tuned by human experts. Human oversight is essential to ensure that the generated plans are consistent with specific organizational needs, account for ethical considerations, and align with the broader strategic vision.

That caveat aside, the planning abilities of large language models empower CEOs to tackle complex decision-making scenarios with greater confidence and efficiency. By understanding the context, identifying goals, and proposing coherent sequences of actions, these models optimize decision-making processes. Their capacity to consider multiple factors, evaluate trade-offs, and iterate on plans offers valuable insights and support in tackling intricate challenges. CEOs who harness the planning abilities of language models can enhance their strategic decision-making, drive organizational success, and unlock unprecedented opportunities.

Applications in Decision-Making

Large language models, with their reasoning and planning capabilities, can become invaluable tools for CEOs in various decision-making contexts. Let's expand on the practical applications of these models in key areas of strategic decision-making.

Strategic Planning

Language models provide significant support in developing long-term strategic plans. By evaluating various scenarios and simulating potential outcomes, these models can assist CEOs in identifying the optimal course of action. They can help analyze market trends, competitive landscape, and potential disruptions to formulate strategies that align with organizational goals.

Moreover, language models can ingest vast amounts of data, including financial reports, industry analysis, and consumer trends. By synthesizing this information, they generate insights that aid in predicting market shifts, identifying emerging opportunities, and formulating adaptive strategies.

Risk Assessment

Language models excel at analyzing data and inferring potential risks, enabling CEOs to anticipate challenges and make informed decisions to mitigate them. These models can analyze complex datasets, including historical data, market trends, and risk indicators, to identify potential areas of vulnerability. CEOs can utilize these insights to proactively address risks, develop mitigation strategies, and ensure business continuity in an economy where downtime can be fatal.

In addition, language models can provide real-time monitoring and analysis of external factors such as geopolitical events, regulatory changes, or market fluctuations. By continuously evaluating the risk landscape, CEOs can respond swiftly to minimize the impact of potential risks on their organizations.

Customer Insights

Language models can analyze customer feedback, reviews, and sentiments to generate valuable insights that not only inform marketing strategies but also product development and customer service improvements. By processing large volumes of data from multiple sources –social media, surveys, customer support interactions, etc. –, these models can identify emerging trends and also customer preferences or areas for improvement.

With these insights, CEOs can, for example, personalize marketing campaigns and optimize product offerings, which enhances customer engagement. Language models can also support sentiment analysis. This allows CEOs to understand customer satisfaction levels, identify potential issues, and take proactive measures to maintain a positive brand reputation.

Supply Chain Optimization

Optimizing supply chain operations is crucial for efficient resource allocation and cost management. Language models can leverage their analytical capabilities to sift through vast amounts of historical data, market trends, and demand forecasts. This enables CEOs to identify patterns, optimize inventory levels, streamline logistics, and minimize supply chain disruptions.

By incorporating language models into supply chain decision-making in this way, CEOs can make data-driven decisions that balance inventory management and customer demand in terms of cost-effectiveness. With correct prompt engineering, these models can factor in variables such as lead times, transportation costs, and supplier performance to optimize procurement strategies and improve overall supply chain efficiency.

Compliance and Regulations

Interpreting complex legal documents and regulatory frameworks can be a daunting task for CEOs. Language models can assist in interpreting such documents, ensuring compliance, and mitigating legal risks. They can analyze legal text to extract key information and provide contextual understanding of specific clauses and requirements.

In addition, CEOs can gain insights into legal implications, assess compliance gaps, and adapt processes and policies accordingly. These models offer efficiency, accuracy, and up-to-date knowledge in navigating complex regulatory landscapes, which reduces the risk of non-compliance and legal consequences.

The possible applications of large language models in decision-making are vast and diverse. From strategic planning and risk assessment to customer insights, supply chain optimization, and compliance, these models provide CEOs with valuable support in making informed decisions. Those who leverage the reasoning and planning capabilities of language models can gain deeper insights, enhance efficiency, and drive their organizations towards success in this ever-evolving business landscape.

Conclusion

In conclusion, large language models offer an unprecedented opportunity for CEOs to revolutionize their decision-making processes and organizations. With their exceptional reasoning and planning capabilities, these models can augment strategic planning efforts, assess risks, derive customer insights, optimize supply chain operations, and ensure compliance with regulations.

CEOs can gain valuable insights from leveraging the language understanding and logical inference capabilities of these models – and therefore make well-informed decisions and navigate complex business landscapes with greater confidence. Having the ability to analyze vast amounts of data, detect patterns, and generate relevant action plans can significantly enhance their problem-solving abilities and drive organizational growth.

The Art and Science of Prompt Engineering with GPT

What is Prompt Engineering and What are its Uses?

PROMPT ENGINEERING IS AN INTEGRAL but often overlooked aspect in the field of artificial intelligence (AI). It pertains to creating effective and seamless cues to instruct models like GPT (Generative Pre-trained Transformer), AI assistants, or chatbots about what is expected of them. Essentially, it's the art of crafting questions or statements to channel the AI output into a desirable direction.

Think of prompt engineering as the hidden choreographer behind a seamlessly executed AI performance; it functions unnoticed in the backdrop, but is absolutely vital to the spectacle. Underpinning distinguished accomplishments in the domain of artificial intelligence (AI), prompt engineering stands as the unsung hero that shapes the direction, defines the pace, and orchestrates the rhythm of every AI interaction.

Like its name suggests, prompt engineering is concentrated around the development of 'prompts': instructions, duties, queries, or tasks, given to the AI models such as General Pre-trained Transformer (GPT), AI assistants, or even chatbots. These prompts form part of the input that AI models receive to generate an output response. To demystify it, think of a person asking their AI assistant to play music, draft an email or remind them about an appointment. In each case, the command given (play music, draft email, set reminder) is the prompt. The more precisely the instruction is articulated, the better the resulting action is likely to be.

At its core, prompt engineering grapples with this very aspect: the art (and indeed, science) of elegantly crafting these questions or statements to guide AI in delivering the most desirable and appropriate output. It's about steering the AI in the right direction, illuminating the path that can best enable our AI assistants to understand and respond to our needs effectively.

This does not mean simply phrasing a clear question or a straightforward task; instead, it pushes further into understanding the intricate workings of AI models and how to optimally engage with them. It involves considering various factors such as context, the order of the statements, the depth of the details, and even the stylistic elements. It is a skill that requires a fine balance between technical knowledge, understanding of natural language, and creativity to rightly tap into the vast capabilities of AI models.

In essence, prompt engineering helps humanize AI interactions. It forms the bridge between the computational language of AI models and the colloquial language of everyday life, making AI a useful, reliable, and accessible tool in our day-to-day operations. Even more so, it is the underpinning framework that allows us to maximize AI's potential and push the boundaries of what can be achieved. We must, therefore, pay heed to this remarkable aspect of AI called prompt engineering.

One way to view prompt engineering is akin to the process of honing a question to get the most desirable answer. When the question or command is clear, precise, and well-structured, the AI model can offer a valuable and accurate response.

It's not just about asking the right question, it's about asking it the right way.

To illustrate, let's ponder upon this scenario. If you're trying to get an assistant to draft an email with the prompt 'Write an email', the response can be quite unpredictable. Add more context, as in 'Write an email to John about the professional development conference next week', and the model's output becomes significantly more accurate and useful. Contextual clarity is key.

When working specifically with OpenAI's API, it is worth noting that GPT, by default, functions like a chat model. This means that placing conversations in your prompts, with 'user' and 'assistant' roles employed alternatively, can optimize the AI's comprehension and subsequent response generation.

For example:

'user': "What's the weather like today?",

'assistant': "Sorry, I am not able to access real-time information."

Including system-level instructions can also be incredibly beneficial to guide the model behavior. Like:

'assistant to=python code': "You can use the `datetime` python module to get the current date and time.", 'assistant': "Sure, here is a sample code for that:

```
import datetime

# Get the current date and time

now = datetime.datetime.now()

print(now)
```
"

This approach, called the 'ChatGPT' style, is preferred for multi-turn conversations and more complex task handling where context accumulation is beneficial.

Another interesting practice is to instruct the model explicitly about the format in which you want the answer. For instance, if you want to write a paragraph about the importance of conservational efforts, the prompt can be 'Explain the importance of conservation efforts in a clear, concise, and informative one-paragraph format.' This guides GPT to provide a succinct and well-formed paragraph about the topic.

In the eventuality where the AI model outputs an unsatisfactory response, it's encouraged to iterate on the task, modify the prompts, and experiment with different approaches, until the output is consistent with the expected results. Remember, every interaction with the model is an opportunity to train it further and fine-tune its capabilities.

Another practice to squeeze the most out of the API is to use 'temperature' and 'max tokens'. While the temperature parameter controls the randomness of the model's output (higher values create more randomness), 'max tokens' restricts the length of the generated content.

Prompts Used for Various AI Tasks

Devising effective prompts is essential to navigating the landscape of various artificial intelligence (AI) tasks. This section aims to demonstrate how prompts play a critical role in diverse tasks. Additionally, it introduces fundamental concepts that hold relevance for the more complex sections of this field.

Let's delve into the details with some examples. For each task, there is an example prompt followed by a prospective model output. This demonstrates the prompt's role as a bridge between AI's computational capabilities and the user's requirement.

Text Summarization

Prompt Example: "Summarize the concept of antibiotics in a succinct and simple language."

Possible Output: "Antibiotics, often prescribed by doctors, are medicines designed to combat bacterial infections. They function by decimating bacteria or inhibiting their growth."

In this scenario, the prompt's straightforward requirement assists the AI in creating a condensed yet comprehensive explanation of antibiotics.

Information Extraction

Prompt Example: "Identify and state the product based on a large language model mentioned in the following paragraph."

Possible Output: "ChatGPT is the large language model-based product referred to in the paragraph."

Here, the AI navigates through the provided text and extracts relevant information guided by the prompt.

Question Answering

Prompt Example: "Using the given context, answer the following question – 'What was the drug approved for?'"

Possible Output: "The drug, as mentioned in the context, was approved to prevent organ rejection following kidney transplantations."

The AI uses the context to provide an accurate response to the query, exhibiting its ability to comprehend and elicit information.

Text Classification

Prompt Example: "Please classify this text into one of the three categories: Neutral, Negative, or Positive."

Possible Output: "The sentiment of the text can be classified as Neutral."

The prompt aids the AI in undertaking sentiment analysis to classify the text according to its emotional hue.

Conversation

Prompt Example: "This is a conversation with an AI research assistant. 'Could you explain black holes?'"

Possible Output: "Black holes are unique areas of spacetime characterized by exceptionally strong gravitational forces, so intense that nothing, including light, can escape from them."

Conversational AI uses the prompts to engage interactively with the users, giving depth and direction to the dialogue.

Code Generation

Prompt Example: "Design code to ask the user for their name and return a greeting saying 'Hello'."

Possible Output:

```
let username = prompt("What is your name?");

console.log(`Hello, ${username}!`);
```

Here, the AI model uses the prompt to generate a basic script in JavaScript, demonstrating its ability to create functional code.

Reasoning

Prompt Example: "Verify if the odd numbers from the following group add up to an even number: 15, 32, 5, 13, 82, 7, 1."

Possible Output: "No, the sum of the odd numbers in the given group (15, 5, 13, 7, 1) results in an odd number, 41."

By evaluating the provided prompt, the AI demonstrates logical reasoning.

These examples underscore the diverse applications of prompts in various AI tasks, showcasing the power and importance of well-structured, intention-driven prompts. They shed light on how effective prompting can elicit desired AI behaviors, making them invaluable tools in AI interactions.

The Crucial Role of Prompt Engineering in Natural Language Processing (NLP) and Artificial Intelligence (AI)

Prompt engineering, within the expansive domains of Natural Language Processing (NLP) and Artificial Intelligence (AI), has rapidly ascended from being an auxiliary function to a vital mechanism. This standing can be attributed to its transformative potential in optimizing and guiding the output generation of language models. Let's dissect the significant contributions of prompt engineering in the world of NLP and AI:

Boosting Model Effectiveness

Modern transformer-based language models, such as GPT, are renowned for their intellectual capabilities. Yet, their broad spectrum intelligence needs competent direction. The role of an aptly designed prompt comes into play here, effectively guiding these models to generate intended outputs. This meticulous choreography ensures that model's prowess is used to its maximum potential – fostering the generation of timely, accurate, and superior responses without the demands of extensive retraining or fine-tuning.

Amplifying Task-Specific Performance

At the heart of AI development is the motive to have machines perform at par and eventually outperform humans. The precise craft of prompt engineering fine-tunes AI models to yield more context-sensitive and nuanced responses, driving their efficiency in specific tasks. Be it language translation, sentiment analysis, or creative text generation, prompt engineering is instrumental in aligning the model's output to the task's nuances.

Deciphering Model Limitations

Exploring prompts offers an insightful perspective into the strengths and weaknesses of a language model. Iterative refinement of prompts and comprehensive evaluation of the model's responses delivers profound understanding. This invaluable insight enhances future model development, functionality expansion, and fosters innovative approaches in NLP.

Assuring Models Safety

AI safety takes a forefront seat when deploying language models to public-centric applications. A carelessly crafted prompt may instigate the model to generate unseemly or harmful content. Prompt engineering comes to the rescue, effectively illuminating the path to prevent such mishaps and offering safer AI model interaction.

Championing Resource Efficiency

Training colossal language models can exert significant demands on computational resources. However, empirical prompt engineering can substantially boost the performance of pre-trained models without the need for additional resource-draining training. Not only does this make AI development more resource-conserving, but it also democratizes access to those with limited computational abilities.

Realizing Domain-Specific Knowledge Transfer

Skilled prompt engineering can infuse language models with industry-specific knowledge, enabling their superior performance in specialized arenas such as healthcare, law, or technology.

Prompt engineering is an integral element to utilize large language models for NLP and a myriad of tasks effectively. It is a lynchpin in heightening model performance, safeguarding AI interactions, economizing resources, and enhancing domain-specific outputs. As we venture further into an era progressively intertwined with AI, the significance of prompt engineering isn't set to diminish, but instead will intensify.

Techniques for Prompt Engineering

Prompt engineering is a rapidly evolving field that utilizes various innovative techniques to optimize the performance of language models. These techniques enable effective communication with large language models, shaping their output, and harnessing their capabilities to their fullest potential. Some of the most useful methods in prompt engineering include:

N-shot prompting

N-shot prompting is a versatile technique in prompt engineering that involves providing examples or cues to guide the language model's predictions. By leveraging these examples, N-shot prompting enables the model to perform tasks even without explicit training on the exact task at hand. It represents a spectrum of approaches, with N indicating the count of examples or cues given to the model.

Zero-shot prompting

Zero-shot prompting is a prominent technique within N-shot prompting. It refers to a situation where the model generates predictions without any explicit, additional examples. In other words, the model is asked to perform a task it has not been explicitly trained on, relying on its general language comprehension and pre-existing knowledge captured during training. This technique is particularly effective for tasks that the model has extensive training for, such as sentiment analysis, spam detection, translation, summarization, and simple text generation. It allows for direct interaction with the model, providing instructions without the need for specific training data.

For example, in zero-shot prompting for sentiment analysis, the model can be prompted with a sentence and asked to classify its sentiment as positive, negative, or neutral. Without providing any explicit training examples, the model can accurately predict the sentiment based on its understanding of sentiments acquired during its initial training. The prompt would look like: "What is the sentiment of the following sentence: 'I had an amazing day at the park'?" The model, drawing on its pre-trained knowledge, would respond with, "The sentiment of the sentence is positive."

Few-shot prompting

Few-shot prompting, on the other hand, involves providing the model with a limited set of examples, typically ranging from two to five, to guide its output. These examples serve as context and provide the model with specific cues to improve its performance in addressing more context-specific problems. Unlike zero-shot prompting, few-shot prompting offers a snapshot of the desired output, allowing the model to tailor its responses more effectively. By incorporating these examples, the model can focus its predictions based on the specific context provided. This technique enhances the accuracy of predictions, especially for tasks where contextual information plays a crucial role.

For instance, in the context of generating a rhymed couplet, a few-shot prompting approach can be used. The model could be prompted with two examples of rhymed couplets about a sunflower and asked to generate a similar rhymed couplet about a moonlit night. The input prompt would look like: "Write a rhymed couplet about a sunflower. Example 1: 'Sunflower with petals bright, Basking gladly in the sunlight.' Example 2: 'Sunflower tall in the summer glow, Nodding as the breezes blow. Now, write a rhymed couplet about a moonlit night.'" By providing these examples, the model gains the necessary context and cues to generate a suitable rhymed couplet about a moonlit night.

N-shot prompting, encompassing both zero-shot and few-shot prompting, highlights the flexibility and adaptability of prompt engineering techniques. It allows for effective communication with the language model, enabling it to generate accurate predictions and responses based on limited or no explicit training on a particular task, ultimately enhancing the model's performance and expanding its range of applications.

Chain-of-thought (CoT) prompting

CoT (Chain-of-thought) prompting represents an innovative technique in prompt engineering that has been developed to enhance the reasoning capabilities of language models. It aims to guide models through the process of solving multi-step problems by encouraging them to reason through intermediate stages. By breaking down complex problems into simpler components, CoT prompting enables models to address challenging reasoning tasks more effectively.

Consider a math word problem as an example. These problems often involve multiple steps and require logical reasoning to arrive at the final answer. By using CoT prompting, the language model is encouraged to dissect the problem into manageable intermediate steps, thereby facilitating a more systematic and organized approach to problem-solving.

Let's take the following math word problem as a scenario: "John has 10 apples. He gives 3 apples to his friend Sam and then buys 6 more apples from the market. How many apples does John have now?"

To solve this problem using CoT prompting, the process would unfold as follows:

1. Initial Prompt: The language model is presented with the first piece of information: "John has 10 apples."

The model utilizes this information to move forward with the problem-solving process.

2. Intermediate Prompt: The model formulates a question based on the intermediate step required to solve the problem: "How many apples does John have if he gives 3 to Sam?"

By introducing this intermediate step, the model initiates a reasoning process to establish the number of apples remaining after the apple transfer.

3. Intermediate Answer: The model generates an intermediate answer based on the reasoning through the given steps: "John has 7 apples."

This answer reflects the outcome of the intermediate step and becomes the foundation for subsequent stages.

4. Intermediate Prompt: The model proceeds to the next intermediate step, considering the new situation: "John has 7 apples."

It formulates a question related to the next action specified in the problem: "How many apples will John have if he buys 6 more apples from the market?"

5. Intermediate Answer: The model generates another intermediate answer that builds upon the previous step: "John has 13 apples."

This answer accounts for the new apples acquired through the purchase.

6. Final Answer: By completing the reasoning through the intermediate steps, the model arrives at the final answer to the original problem: "John has 13 apples now."

The model's ability to reason through the steps and integrate intermediate answers ultimately allows it to determine the solution to the entire problem.

CoT prompting breaks down complex problems into simpler sub-problems, facilitating the model's ability to reason through each step and build upon previously solved sub-problems. This approach mimics the way humans tackle multifaceted problems, allowing models to better understand and address challenging reasoning tasks.

By employing CoT prompting, language models gain improved problem-solving capabilities, enhancing their overall understanding of complex tasks. The technique enables models to dissect intricate problems into manageable components, leading to more effective reasoning, accurate predictions, and insightful responses, even in scenarios involving multiple steps and complex reasoning pathways.

Self-consistency prompting

Self-consistency prompting is an advanced variation of the Chain-of-thought (CoT) prompting technique that focuses on generating multiple diverse reasoning paths and selecting answers that demonstrate the highest level of consistency. It aims to enhance precision, reliability, and confidence in the model's responses by employing a consensus-based system.

In self-consistency prompting, the language model is encouraged to explore various reasoning paths, considering different factors and viewpoints. By generating multiple paths, the model can provide a range of possible answers and evaluate their alignment with each other. The goal is to identify the answers that exhibit the highest level of internal consistency, ensuring that they are reliable and dependable.

Let's delve into an example to illustrate how self-consistency prompting works. Imagine you want to use self-consistency prompting in a scenario involving decision-making for selecting the best holiday destination. Several factors are considered, such as budget, proximity, weather, and activities. The resulting question could be: "What would be the best holiday destination considering a budget of $3000, a preference for warm weather, and a love for beach activities?"

To utilize self-consistency prompting in this context, the model generates multiple reasoning paths, each exploring how different factors might inform the answer:

Path 1:

- Initial prompt: "Considering a budget of $3000 and a preference for warm weather."

- Intermediate answer: "A tropical destination would fit these criteria. Let's consider Bali."

- Following prompt: "What about considering beach activities?"

- Final answer: "Bali is renowned for its beach activities. So, it could be the best choice."

Path 2:

- Initial prompt: "Considering a preference for warm weather and a love for beach activities."

- Intermediate answer: "Hawaii is well-known for its excellent weather and beach activities."

- Following prompt: "Considering a budget of $3000, is Hawaii a good choice?"

- Final answer: "Yes, Hawaii could be a great choice considering all three factors."

Path 3:

- Initial prompt: "Considering a budget of $3000 and a love for beach activities."

- Intermediate answer: "Considering these factors, the Bahamas could be a great destination."

- Following prompt: "Considering a preference for warm weather, is the Bahamas a good choice?"

- Final answer: "Indeed, the Bahamas is known for its warm weather. So, it could be the best choice."

In this scenario, the model generates distinct reasoning paths based on the provided criteria. Each reasoning path suggests a potential destination that aligns with different combinations of budget, weather, and activities. The model ensures consistency within each path by considering the factors comprehensively.

To make a decision, a majority voting system can be applied. The most consistent answer among the reasoning paths is chosen as the final output of the self-consistency prompting process. The diversity in the prompts ensures a comprehensive assessment, and the most consistent destination can be considered the most suitable option considering the provided conditions.

By incorporating self-consistency prompting, the language model gains the ability to generate multiple reasoning paths, providing a range of potential answers and evaluating their internal consistency. This consensus-based approach enhances precision, reliability, and trustworthiness in the model's responses, making it a valuable technique in prompt engineering for decision-making scenarios where multiple factors have to be considered.

Least-to-most prompting (LtM)

Least-to-most prompting (LtM) is a powerful technique in prompt engineering that aims to break down complex problems into a series of less complex sub-problems, which are then solved sequentially. It mimics the teaching strategies employed in real-world scenarios, where educators guide learners through step-by-step problem-solving processes. By leveraging LtM prompting, language models can tackle multifaceted problems more effectively and arrive at accurate solutions.

To illustrate how LtM prompting works, let's consider an example involving a math word problem. Math word problems often present challenges as they require understanding the problem context, identifying relevant information, and applying appropriate mathematical operations to find the solution. LtM prompting assists the language model in navigating these complex problems systematically.

Suppose the math word problem is as follows: "John has twice as many apples as Jane. Jane has 5 apples. How many apples does John have?"

Here's how LtM prompting can be applied to break down the problem into simpler sub-problems:

First Sub-problem:

- Initial prompt: "Jane has 5 apples."

- Intermediate answer: "So, the number of apples Jane has is 5."

Second Sub-problem:

- Initial prompt: "John has twice as many apples as Jane."

- Intermediate answer: "So, John has 2 times the number of apples that Jane has."

Third Sub-problem:

- Initial prompt: "Given that Jane has 5 apples and John has twice as many apples as Jane, how many apples does John have?"

- Final answer: "John has 2 * 5 = 10 apples."

In LtM prompting, each sub-problem is designed to be less complex than the original problem. The model solves these sub-problems sequentially, with each subsequent sub-problem building upon the solutions obtained from previously addressed sub-problems. By breaking down the problem into manageable steps, the model gains a clearer understanding of the task at hand and can generate accurate solutions more effectively.

The strength of LtM prompting lies in its ability to simplify complex problems by dividing them into more manageable components, just like how learners grasp concepts incrementally. By following this step-by-step approach, language models are able to reason through each sub-problem and leverage the solutions obtained in previous steps to guide their progress. This not only enhances their problem-solving capabilities but also promotes a deeper understanding of the problem context, leading to more accurate and reliable final answers.

Overall, LtM prompting is a valuable technique in prompt engineering, enabling language models to handle complex problem-solving tasks by breaking them down into simpler stages, similar to real-world teaching strategies.

Active prompting

Active prompting is a dynamic technique in prompt engineering that aims to enhance model accuracy by identifying uncertain questions and annotating them with human expertise. This approach involves selecting questions for human annotation based on the model's uncertainty in its predictions. By integrating the annotated data back into the prompt, the model can improve its understanding and generate more informed and accurate responses.

Let's consider an example to illustrate how active prompting works in the context of a language model engaged in a conversation about climate change. Imagine a scenario where the model engages in a back-and-forth conversation with the user, answering questions and providing information related to climate change. Throughout the conversation, the model identifies questions that it is uncertain about and would benefit from additional annotation.

For instance, imagine the model encounters the following potential questions with varying levels of uncertainty:

1. "What is the average global temperature?"

2. "What are the primary causes of global warming?"

3. "How does carbon dioxide contribute to the greenhouse effect?"

In this scenario, the model might be relatively confident about the answers to the first two questions since they are common questions about the topic. However, the third question about carbon dioxide's contribution to the greenhouse effect might present some uncertainty to the model.

Active prompting would identify the third question as the most uncertain and valuable for human annotation. The model would select this question and send it for human annotation. An expert or annotator would provide the model with the information necessary to correctly answer the question. The annotated question and answer would then be integrated back into the model's prompt, enabling it to handle similar questions with improved accuracy in the future.

The process of active prompting helps address uncertainties and knowledge gaps by leveraging human expertise to provide more accurate and reliable answers. By selecting questions that pose the highest uncertainty and involving human annotators, the model can augment its understanding and knowledge base. This iterative process of incorporating annotated data enhances the model's comprehension and enables it to generate more informed, contextually aware, and precise responses.

Active prompting is particularly valuable in dynamic domains where new information emerges, or where the model's training data does not cover all possible scenarios. By actively seeking human annotation to address uncertainties, the model becomes more adaptable and capable of providing reliable information in real-world contexts.

Overall, active prompting is an effective approach in prompt engineering that utilizes human annotation to improve model accuracy and address uncertainties. By identifying uncertain questions and integrating annotated data, the model gains a deeper understanding of complex topics, ensuring more reliable and informative responses.

Generated knowledge prompting

Generated knowledge prompting is a powerful technique in prompt engineering that capitalizes on a language model's ability to generate informative knowledge related to a given prompt. It leverages the model's vast language comprehension and training to produce contextual and precise responses with relevant information. By incorporating the generated knowledge into subsequent prompts, models can provide more informed, accurate, and contextually aware answers.

To illustrate how generated knowledge prompting works, let's consider an example that involves using a language model to provide answers to complex technical questions, specifically related to quantum entanglement and its application in quantum computing.

Suppose the question is: "Can you explain how quantum entanglement works in quantum computing?"

In this scenario, generated knowledge prompting would involve two steps:

1. Prompt for generating an overview: The language model is initially prompted with a broader question to generate an informative overview or explanation of the topic. For example: "Provide an overview of quantum entanglement."

The model then draws on its pre-trained knowledge and understanding of the topic to generate a response that provides a detailed explanation of quantum entanglement. This generated overview encapsulates the foundational concepts, mechanisms, and principles associated with quantum entanglement.

2. Prompt for a specific question based on the generated knowledge: Building on the knowledge generated in the previous step, a more specific question is formulated to delve deeper into the application of quantum entanglement in quantum computing. For example: "Given that quantum entanglement involves the instantaneous connection between two particles regardless of distance, how does this concept apply in quantum computing?"

By incorporating the generated knowledge about quantum entanglement into the prompt, the model is prompted to provide a more focused and informed response specific to the application of quantum entanglement in the context of quantum computing. The model can then draw upon its understanding of the topic, combined with the generated knowledge, to provide a more precise and accurate answer that aligns with the specific question.

Generated knowledge prompting enhances the model's ability to produce informed responses that are grounded in relevant information. By first generating a comprehensive overview and then utilizing this knowledge in subsequent prompts, the model demonstrates a more contextual understanding of the topic. This technique enables the model to provide more detailed, accurate, and insightful responses that go beyond simple generative language capabilities.

Overall, generated knowledge prompting empowers language models to go beyond general language comprehension and generate informative knowledge about specific topics. By incorporating this generated knowledge into subsequent prompts, models can produce more contextually aware and precise answers, enhancing their performance in tasks that require deep understanding and expertise.

Directional stimulus prompting

Directional stimulus prompting is a powerful technique in prompt engineering that directs the response of a language model in a specific manner. By providing clear instructions and guidelines within the prompt, this technique guides the model to generate output that aligns closely with the desired format, structure, tone, or objective. Directional stimulus prompts enable precise control over the model's output, ensuring that it produces responses that meet specific criteria.

An example of directional stimulus prompting is when we want the language model to generate a concise summary of a given text in a single sentence suitable for a headline. This prompts the model to condense the main points, essence, or key message of the text into a succinct and attention-grabbing summary.

To achieve this, instead of a generic prompt like "Summarize this article," a directional stimulus prompt would provide clearer instructions. For instance, the prompt could be: "Summarize this article in a single sentence that could be used as a headline."

By including this additional instruction, the model is directed to generate a summary with specific criteria, such as being succinct, attention-grabbing, and suitable for a headline. This guidance ensures that the model's response aligns closely with the intended purpose or context of the summary, meeting the requirement of a concise and compelling headline.

This technique is not limited to summarization tasks but can be employed in various other scenarios where specific output requirements are desired. For example, in the context of generating rhymes, instead of a generic prompt like "Generate a rhyme," a directional stimulus prompt might be: "Generate a rhyme in the style of Dr. Seuss about friendship." This instruction guides the model to produce a rhyme that adheres to the specific style of Dr. Seuss and revolves around the theme of friendship, resulting in a more targeted and desired response.

Directional stimulus prompting empowers prompt engineers to have precise control over the output of language models. By providing clear instructions and specific guidelines in the prompts, the potential for generating responses that meet specific criteria or objectives is maximized. This technique enables efficient communication with the model and allows fine-tuning of the output to match specific requirements, making it a valuable tool in prompt engineering.

ReAct prompting

ReAct (Reasoning and Acting) prompting is a cutting-edge technique in prompt engineering that combines verbal reasoning with interactive actions to enhance the capabilities of language models. This approach goes beyond traditional prompting methods by allowing models to dynamically reason and adapt their plans while engaging with external environments. By seamlessly integrating verbal reasoning and physical actions, ReAct prompting enables models to generate more accurate, comprehensive, and informed responses to complex tasks.

To illustrate how ReAct prompting works, let's consider an example involving a language model tasked with creating a detailed report on the current state of artificial intelligence (AI). In this scenario, the model is prompted to not only generate verbal reasoning traces but also perform real-world actions related to the task.

Here's how ReAct prompting can unfold to complete this task:

Step 1: Reasoning Stage

The language model starts the process by comprehending the prompt, which requires it to create a detailed report on AI. The model generates verbal reasoning traces, mentally mapping out the steps it needs to take to accomplish the task.

Step 2: Action Stage

The model transitions from verbal reasoning to active involvement. It performs specific actions related to the task, such as fetching the latest AI research papers from a database, querying for recent news on AI from reputable sources, or accessing relevant information from information-rich sites like Wikipedia.

Step 3: Interaction Stage

The actions performed by the model in the previous stage lead to an interaction with external environments. For instance, if the model accessed a database or queried news sources, it receives the most up-to-date research papers and news articles on AI.

Step 4: Reasoning and Acting Integration

With the acquired information, the model combines verbal reasoning and the input from external environments. It dynamically reasons through the obtained data, adapts its plans, and generates a more accurate and comprehensive report on the current state of AI.

The combination of reasoning and acting in ReAct prompting allows the model to leverage its language comprehension and cognitive abilities while augmenting its knowledge with real-world interactions. By interacting with external environments, the model gains access to the most recent and relevant information, improving the accuracy and depth of its report. This hybrid approach enhances the model's understanding and problem-solving capabilities, overcoming limitations seen in previous prompting methods.

ReAct prompting enables language models to dynamically adapt their plans and thinking patterns, resembling how humans learn new tasks and make decisions by reasoning and acting in interactive environments. By integrating verbal reasoning and physical actions in a seamless manner, the models become more proficient in addressing complex tasks and generating comprehensive and informed responses.

Overall, ReAct prompting represents an innovative technique in prompt engineering that combines reasoning and acting to enhance the accuracy, depth, and problem-solving capabilities of language models. By enabling models to interact with external environments and dynamically adapt their plans while generating verbal reasoning traces, ReAct prompting pushes the boundaries of what models can achieve in a diverse range of tasks and applications.

Multimodal CoT prompting

Multimodal CoT (Chain-of-thought) prompting is an advanced technique in prompt engineering that builds upon the fundamental principles of CoT prompting. It extends the approach by incorporating both textual and visual information, enabling language models to reason and generate responses that involve complex interactions between text and images. By leveraging multimodal data, models can produce more accurate, contextually relevant, and comprehensive responses that take into account information from both modalities.

To illustrate how multimodal CoT prompting works, let's consider an example involving the identification of a bird in an image. The prompt requires the model to utilize textual information about bird species and visual cues from the provided image to generate a response that correctly identifies the bird.

Here's how multimodal CoT prompting can be applied to identify a bird in an image:

Step 1: Reasoning about Visual Features

The language model is prompted with an image of a bird, and it begins the reasoning process by analyzing the distinguishing visual features of the bird. This may include characteristics such as color, size, beak shape, patterns, or specific markers.

Step 2: Cross-referencing with Textual Bird Species Information

Drawing upon its pre-trained textual knowledge about various bird species, the model cross-references the visual features identified in the image with the characteristics described in the textual bird species information. It matches the visual cues to potential bird species that exhibit similar attributes.

Step 3: Integration and Final Answer

By synthesizing the visual features identified in the image and the textual bird species information, the model generates a response that accurately identifies the bird. This response combines the visual analysis with the textual knowledge, producing a contextually relevant and informed answer.

The multimodal CoT prompting technique allows language models to reason through both textual and visual information, mimicking how humans integrate multiple modalities to make informed judgments. By leveraging the synergies between text and images, models can generate responses that are more comprehensive, accurate, and contextually nuanced.

The incorporation of visual data in multimodal CoT prompting enables models to solve problems that require reasoning about both text and images. This technique finds applications in various domains, such as image classification, visual question answering, image captioning, and more. It empowers models to interpret and reason with multimodal inputs, resulting in a richer understanding of complex tasks and more precise responses.

Multimodal CoT prompting demonstrates the potential for language models to leverage both textual and visual information, allowing them to perform complex reasoning tasks that involve multiple modalities. By integrating the power of language understanding with visual perception, these models can bridge the gap between different forms of data, leading to more sophisticated and comprehensive AI capabilities.

Graph prompting

Graph prompting is an advanced technique in prompt engineering that leverages the structure and content of graphs to guide language models in their responses. It involves translating graph data into a format that the model can comprehend and process. By using graph prompts, language models can effectively tackle question-answering and problem-solving tasks that rely on relationships and connections within a graph.

To illustrate graph prompting, let's consider an example involving a social network graph. Suppose we have a graph that represents relationships between individuals, where nodes represent people and edges represent friendships. The task is to identify the person with the most connections or friends within the network.

Graph prompting involves converting the graph data into a format suitable for the language model. Instead of directly providing the graph itself, a prompt is constructed that highlights the essential relationships and information from the graph. This prompt acts as a guide for the model to navigate and reason through the underlying graph structure.

For example, the prompt may include a list of friendships as a textual representation of graph connections. It could look like this: "Alice is friends with Bob. Bob is friends with Charlie. Alice is friends with Charlie."

The language model, utilizing this graph prompt, can then reason and analyze the provided friend relationships to identify the person with the most connections. By comprehending the graph relationships through the prompt, the model can determine the individual(s) who appear multiple times as friends and, thus, have the most connections within the social network.

Graph prompting allows language models to handle complex graph-related tasks and reason through the intricate connections between entities. It enables models to analyze relationships, identify patterns, and make inferences based on the given graph data. By providing a structured and accessible representation of graph information, graph prompting facilitates effective communication and interaction between language models and graph-based systems.

Overall, graph prompting is a valuable technique in prompt engineering that enables language models to tackle questions and solve problems based on graph relationships. By translating the graph into a format the model can understand, graph prompting empowers models to reason through complex graph structures, bridging the gap between structured data and natural language processing, and facilitating insightful and accurate responses.

These prompt engineering techniques are powerful tools to optimize the performance and capabilities of language models, making them more sophisticated and adaptable for a wide range of tasks and applications.

Tree of Thought Model

Beyond the realms of traditional prompt engineering, a new innovative concept coined as the "Tree of Thought" model garners attention. Rooted in the core constructs of conversational AI, the Tree of Thought model presents a unique and interactive method for communicating with AI models.

In the Tree of Thought model, imagine the conversational exchanges between the user and the AI as branches that grow from a central trunk, which represents the main conversation. These branches are not just linear offshoots but can split, converge, and extend in various directions, forming new "thoughts." Each branch is an idea or a topic that can independently evolve, yet collectively influence the overall dialog.

Now, let's elucidate this with an example. If we're talking about 'recent technological advancements' and that sparks a sub-conversation about 'AI in healthcare', this new topic can be seen as a branch extending from our conversation's main trunk. As we delve deeper into 'AI in healthcare', further branches may form, discussing AI usage in disease prediction, patient care, data management, etc.

The power of the Tree of Thought model arises in its ability to track and manage the development of these different branches effectively. It becomes an architectural map of the ongoing dialog, keeping track of multiple evolving threads while staying rooted in the main conversation.

This model is especially beneficial when working with AI models like GPT, where context management is crucial. By representing the context as a series of branching thoughts, the model can more effectively manage different dialog threads, retain context over extended interactions, and navigate back to previous topics when needed. The Tree of Thought model allows AI to associate, differentiate and reconnect various segments of conversation, thereby providing a holistic and engaging conversational experience.

Overall, the Tree of Thought model represents an evolutionary leap in prompt engineering. It not only enhances the conceptual organization of dialogues but also unlocks the potential for AI models to handle more intricate, extended, and context-dependent interactions. It brings us a step closer to making AI dialogs as fluid, dynamic, and enjoyable as human conversations.

The Step-by-Step Process of Prompt Engineering

Prompt engineering involves a multi-step process with several key tasks. Here's a breakdown of each step:

Step 1: Understanding the Problem

Understanding the problem is the fundamental step in prompt engineering and sets the stage for crafting effective prompts. It involves gaining a comprehensive understanding of what needs to be accomplished and delving into the underlying structure and nuances of the task. This understanding allows prompt engineers to tailor the prompts specifically to achieve the desired outcomes.

When approaching prompt engineering, it is vital to consider the type of problem being addressed. Different types of problems require different prompts to guide the model effectively. For example, question-answering tasks necessitate prompts that retrieve or generate accurate answers to specific queries. Understanding the types of information required in the answers, such as factual, analytical, or subjective, helps in crafting the appropriate prompts.

Text generation tasks require prompts that provide guidance on creating coherent and contextually appropriate textual responses. When formulating prompts for text generation, factors such as the desired length of the output, the specific format (e.g., story, poem, article), and the intended tone or style play a crucial role in guiding the model.

Sentiment analysis tasks require prompts that enable the model to discern and evaluate the sentiment expressed in text. Prompts should be designed to guide the model in identifying and analyzing subjective expressions accurately. Understanding the nature and nuances of sentiment analysis helps prompt engineers develop prompts that elicit the desired sentiment-based responses.

Furthermore, understanding the potential challenges and limitations associated with the task is an important aspect of problem analysis. These challenges could include domain-specific language, cultural references, or variations in expression that the model may encounter. By anticipating and addressing these challenges in the prompt, prompt engineers can help guide the model to produce more accurate and relevant responses.

A deep understanding of the problem also allows prompt engineers to anticipate how the model might react to different prompts. It provides insights into the potential pitfalls and limitations of the model and helps guide the selection of appropriate prompts to mitigate these challenges.

Problem analysis is a combination of art and science, requiring both technical expertise and a broader understanding of the task at hand. Prompt engineers must invest time in studying the problem domain, examining relevant datasets, reviewing existing literature, and consulting domain experts if necessary. This comprehensive understanding of the problem enables prompt engineers to identify the key parameters and requirements that the prompt must capture accurately.

The more deeply prompt engineers comprehend the problem and its nuances, the better-equipped they are to craft prompts that are precise, effective, and able to elicit the desired responses from the model. Understanding the problem domain is the foundation of prompt engineering and sets the path for successful prompt design and development.

Step 2: Crafting the Initial Prompt

Crafting the initial prompt is a crucial step in prompt engineering as it sets the foundation for directing the language model. The goal is to create instructions that are clear, concise, and unambiguous, ensuring that the model understands the intended task and produces the desired output.

The prompt should provide explicit guidance to the model, outlining the specific requirements and objectives. It should communicate the expected format, tone, or style of the response, depending on the task at hand.

For example, if the task involves text generation, the prompt should specify factors such as the desired length of the output, the genre or format (story, poem, article), and the tone (formal or informal).

Including few-shot examples within the initial prompt can further enhance the model's understanding and context. These examples serve as concrete illustrations of the expected input and output. By providing specific instances, the model can grasp the patterns, structure, and nuances required to generate accurate responses. For instance, if the prompt aims to teach the model to translate English text into French, including a few examples of English sentences and their corresponding French translations can help the model comprehend the desired translation patterns and context.

Prompts should be designed with flexibility in mind. It is unlikely that the ideal output will be achieved with the first prompt attempt. Iteration and refinement are often necessary to refine the instructions and improve the model's performance. As the model generates responses based on the initial prompt, the outcomes should be evaluated, and any areas of misalignment or shortcomings should be identified. This feedback loop informs the prompt engineering process, allowing for adjustments and improvements to be made.

During the crafting process, it's important to consider the language and tone used in the prompt. Clear and straightforward language enhances the model's understanding and reduces the chances of misinterpretation. Additionally, the prompt should provide guidance that is comprehensive and covers all essential aspects of the task. It should address potential challenges, like domain-specific language, slang, or cultural references, to ensure that the model can handle such complexities.

Crafting the initial prompt is a delicate balance between providing sufficient guidance to the model while also allowing room for creativity and adaptation. It necessitates constant evaluation, refinement, and optimization to ensure that the instructions effectively steer the model towards producing accurate and meaningful responses.

Step 3: Evaluating the Model's Response

Once the model has generated a response based on the initial prompt, it is essential to evaluate the output to assess its alignment with the intended goal of the task. Evaluating the model's response allows for an in-depth analysis of its performance and understanding of the prompt.

The primary objective of this evaluation is to determine whether the model's response meets the desired outcome. It involves assessing various aspects, including relevance, accuracy, completeness, and contextual understanding.

Relevance: Evaluate whether the model's response is relevant to the given task. Does it directly address the question or problem posed in the prompt, or does it veer off-topic? Ensuring relevance is crucial for achieving the desired outcome.

Accuracy: Consider the accuracy of the information provided in the model's response. Is it factually correct? Does it provide accurate analysis or insights? Accuracy is especially important in tasks that require precise and reliable information, such as question-answering or data analysis.

Completeness: Determine if the model's response is comprehensive and complete. Does it cover all aspects of the task or question? Ensure that the response encompasses all relevant details and information required for a thorough and informative output.

Contextual Understanding: Evaluate the model's ability to grasp and comprehend the context provided in the prompt. Is it able to capture the nuances and intricacies of the given context, or does it produce responses that lack contextual coherence? Contextual understanding is crucial for generating accurate and contextually relevant outputs.

Identifying areas of discrepancy is a vital part of the evaluation process. If the model's response falls short in any of the evaluation measures, it is important to understand why. Discrepancies may arise due to various factors such as the prompt not being explicit enough, the task being too complex for the model's existing capabilities, or insufficient training data for the specific task. Pinpointing the shortcomings helps to determine where improvements are needed, both in the prompt itself and in the model's training.

Effectively evaluating the model's response enables a deeper understanding of its performance and limitations. This understanding helps inform the next step in prompt engineering: refining the prompt. By identifying gaps and areas for improvement, prompt engineers can make the necessary adjustments to enhance the prompt and guide the model towards producing more accurate and desired responses.

Throughout the prompt engineering process, the evaluation stage acts as a feedback loop, providing valuable insights that inform prompt adjustments, model training, and overall optimization. Continuous evaluation and refinement are crucial to ensuring that the prompt and model work together effectively to achieve the desired outcomes.

Step 4: Iterating and Refining the Prompt

After evaluating the model's response and identifying areas for improvement, the next step in prompt engineering is to iterate and refine the prompt. This iterative process involves making adjustments to the prompt based on the insights gained from the evaluation.

One key aspect of iterating and refining the prompt is to ensure that the instructions are clear, concise, and unambiguous. If the model struggled with explicit guidance or produced inaccurate responses, it is important to revisit the prompt instructions. Simplify or rephrase the instructions to make them more specific and easily comprehensible for the model. Clarity in the prompt instructions reduces the chances of misinterpretation by the language model and guides it towards generating more accurate and desired responses.

Another approach to refining the prompt is to provide more examples within the prompt itself. Adding additional illustrative examples helps the model understand the desired structure or required output better. These examples act as guidelines, demonstrating the correct form, substance, or style of the expected response. By including more examples, prompt engineers can enhance the model's ability to generate outputs that align with the desired objectives of the task.

Moreover, altering the format or structure of the prompt can also be effective in refining the prompt. Experimenting with different sentence order, phrasing, or organization can lead to improved response quality. For example, reordering the questions or breaking them down into smaller, more digestible parts can assist the model in understanding the prompt more accurately. Additionally, adding specific keywords or format cues can guide the model towards generating responses that adhere to the desired format or structure.

The process of iterating and refining the prompt is typically conducted through multiple rounds. After making adjustments to the prompt, the model is reevaluated, and its responses are analyzed once again. This iterative cycle allows for continuous improvement and fine-tuning of the prompt, resulting in better alignment with the desired outputs.

It's important to note that prompt refinement is not a linear process. It requires adaptability and flexibility. Different prompt adjustments might be necessary depending on the model's response and the specific requirements of the task. Through careful iteration and refining, prompt engineers can actively address shortcomings and enhance the prompt's ability to guide the model effectively.

The iterative and refining step of prompt engineering is where considerable effort is dedicated to optimizing the prompt to achieve the desired outcome. By continuously iterating and refining the prompt based on the model's responses, prompt engineers can ensure that the instructions guide the model towards generating accurate, coherent, and contextually appropriate outputs.

Step 5: Testing the Prompt on Different Models

After refining the prompt, it is essential to test its performance on various models to gain insights into its robustness and generalizability. Different models may have different architectures, training methodologies, or datasets, which can influence their understanding and response to a given prompt. Testing the prompt across a range of models helps provide a comprehensive assessment of its effectiveness and versatility.

One of the main objectives of testing the prompt on different models is to evaluate its performance consistency. By applying the prompt to various models, prompt engineers can determine if the desirable results achieved with one model can be consistently reproduced across different models. This insight into the prompt's performance consistency allows for a more accurate assessment of its effectiveness and aids in identifying any potential limitations or model-specific considerations.

During this testing phase, it is crucial to assess how well the prompt performs on different models by examining various aspects, including relevance, accuracy, completeness, and contextual understanding. Comparing the model responses helps reveal differences in performance, shedding light on how different characteristics of the models, such as architecture or training data, affect their understanding and output.

The size of the model is an important consideration during the testing process. Larger models often have a broader context window and advanced capabilities, enabling them to generate more nuanced responses. However, smaller models may require more explicit prompting due to their limited contextual understanding. By testing the prompt on models of varying sizes, prompt engineers can gain insights into the optimal model size required for the prompt to achieve the desired outcome.

Furthermore, the architecture of the models plays a significant role in how they process and respond to prompts. Some architectures excel at specific tasks, while others may struggle. By testing the prompt on models with different architectures, it becomes possible to understand how the prompt performs on each architecture and which models are best suited for the given task.

It is also important to consider the training data of the models during testing. Models trained on a wide range of topics and genres tend to provide more versatile responses, while models trained on specific domains or specialized datasets might have limitations in handling broader or unfamiliar prompts. By testing the prompt on models with different training data, prompt engineers can assess the impact of the training data on the model's response quality.

Ultimately, testing the prompt on different models helps refine its design and make it adaptable to various scenarios and requirements. Insights gained during this phase enable prompt engineers to make necessary adjustments or refinements to the prompt, ensuring its effectiveness and generality across a wider range of large language models.

This testing process is essential for prompt engineering and reinforces the versatility and applicability of the prompt across different models. It aids in optimizing the prompt's performance, allowing it to effectively guide models and AI assistants in generating accurate and meaningful responses across various platforms and contexts.

Step 6: Scaling the Prompt

After refining the prompt and ensuring its consistent production of desirable results, the next step in prompt engineering is to scale its utility. Scaling involves extending the prompt's application across broader contexts, tasks, or automation levels. This process enables the prompt to be deployed in real-world applications and maximizes its efficiency and effectiveness.

One way to scale the prompt is by automating the prompt generation process. Automation can significantly save time, especially when dealing with a high volume of tasks or data. By creating scripts or tools that automate the prompt generation based on certain parameters or rules, the process becomes streamlined and efficient. Automation also reduces the chances of human error in manually crafting prompts and ensures consistency in the prompt generation process. Automating prompt generation enables prompt engineers to rapidly apply the prompt to new tasks, making it a scalable solution.

Another approach to scaling the prompt is by creating variations of the prompt to address related tasks. Leveraging the foundational work already done in crafting the original prompt, variations can be tailored to different domains, topics, or specific requirements. For example, if a prompt successfully guides a model in sentiment analysis for product reviews, variations of this prompt can be created to apply it to movie reviews, book reviews, or restaurant reviews. By adapting the prompt to similar tasks, prompt engineers can save time and effort while addressing a wider range of applications. Variations allow for quick and efficient adaptation of the foundational prompt to related tasks, expanding its applicability and ensuring its versatility.

Scaling the prompt represents a successful transition from the development phase to the deployment phase. It indicates that the prompt has been refined and tested to a point where it consistently produces desirable results. The scaled prompt is ready to be used in real-world applications on a broader scale, addressing an array of contexts, tasks, or automation levels.

It is worth noting that scaling the prompt requires ongoing monitoring and evaluation to ensure its continued success. As the prompt is employed in different contexts and scenarios, prompt engineers should assess its performance, gather feedback, and make necessary adjustments to further optimize its effectiveness. The iterative nature of prompt engineering continues even at the scaling stage, as real-world deployment may present new challenges and opportunities for refinement.

Scaling the prompt contributes to the efficiency and effectiveness of AI systems by providing a reusable blueprint that can be utilized across different applications. It allows for prompt engineering to have a broader impact, facilitating the deployment of AI solutions with consistent and reliable performance.

Overall, scaling the prompt is a crucial step in prompt engineering, involving the automation of prompt generation and the creation of variations to address related tasks. This step ensures the prompt's wider applicability, consistency, and versatility in real-world applications, ultimately maximizing its value and impact.

Remember, prompt engineering is an ongoing iterative process. Continuous testing, refinement, and optimization are required to achieve optimal performance and adapt to changing requirements.

Essential Components of an Effective Prompt

When delving into the realm of prompt engineering, we come across four key elements that serve as the foundation for this field. These elements, namely instructions, context, input data, and output indicators, play a crucial role in facilitating effective communication with large language models. By understanding and skillfully utilizing these components, you can shape the responses of AI models and guide their operations. In the following section, we will delve into each of these elements, equipping you with the knowledge to apply them efficiently on your AI development journey.

Instructions

Instructions are a fundamental component of a prompt, serving as the foundation for guiding an AI model's behavior. They provide a clear and concise directive that outlines the desired task to be performed by the model. The instruction sets the overall objective and acts as a guidepost for the model's decision-making process.

When crafting instructions, it is crucial to be specific and unambiguous, leaving no room for misunderstanding. Well-defined instructions allow the model to comprehend the task at hand and generate responses that align with the desired outcome. For instance, if the instruction is to translate a text into French, the model understands that its purpose is to convert the given text from one language to another.

Instructions can vary greatly depending on the complexity and specificity of the task. They may involve tasks such as summarization, sentiment analysis, question-answering, or even more creative endeavors like story generation. For example, instructing the model to generate ideas for a science fiction story prompts it to tap into its knowledge and generative capabilities to propose compelling plotlines, unique characters, and captivating settings.

To enhance the effectiveness of instructions, it is often beneficial to provide additional details, constraints, or examples when necessary. This helps the model grasp the specific requirements of the task and produce more accurate and tailored responses. By incorporating relevant information into the instructions, such as the intended audience, desired tone, or specific context, you can guide the model's understanding and influence its creative output.

Moreover, instructions can also include elements that guide the model's decision-making process, such as indicating the criteria to be considered in the response generation. This helps the model prioritize relevant information and produce outputs that are aligned with the desired goal.

Overall, instructions play a pivotal role in prompt engineering by setting the stage and providing a clear objective for the model. By carefully crafting instructions, you can ensure that the model understands the task, focuses its efforts in the right direction, and generates responses that meet your specific requirements.

Context

Context plays a crucial role in prompt engineering by providing the necessary background information that aids the AI model in generating more accurate and contextually appropriate responses. By offering supplementary details, the context enhances the model's understanding of the task, enabling it to produce outputs that align with the desired style, tone, and specific nuances.

In a translation task, context can include various elements that provide a deeper understanding of the text to be translated. For example, you might specify that the source text is a movie dialogue, indicating to the model that it needs to consider conversational language and casual expressions commonly found in film scripts. On the other hand, if the source text is a passage from a scientific paper, the context informs the model to adopt a more formal and technical tone in the translated output.

Context can also encompass information about the subject matter, the intended audience, or any cultural references that may be relevant to the task. For instance, if the translation involves a specific field like medical or legal documents, providing contextual details helps the model in using domain-specific terminology and ensuring accurate translations within that specialized subject area.

By including context in the prompt, prompt engineers can steer the AI model towards generating responses that are more meaningful and contextually appropriate. This enables the model to grasp the intended meaning and purpose behind the task, leading to more accurate translations or informative outputs.

Furthermore, context can be utilized to guide the model's decision-making process by emphasizing particular aspects of the input data. For instance, in a text generation task, providing context about the desired genre, narrative style, or point of view can direct the model in crafting responses that adhere to those specific requirements.

Overall, context serves as a critical component in prompt engineering as it enhances the model's comprehension of the task, allowing it to generate responses that reflect the desired style, tone, and contextual nuances. By providing sufficient background information, prompt engineers can guide the model's understanding and ensure its outputs are contextually accurate, consistent, and purposeful.

Input data

Input data forms the raw material that an AI model processes and uses as the foundation for generating responses. It is the actual information or data that the model works with to perform the desired task. The specific type and format of the input data may vary depending on the nature of the task at hand.

For example, in a translation task, the input data consists of the text that needs to be translated from one language to another. This could be a sentence, a paragraph, or an entire document. The model analyzes this input data, applies its language processing capabilities, and generates a translated version of the provided text.

In a question-answering task, the input data is typically the question being posed to the model. This question serves as the input that triggers the model to search and process the relevant information needed to generate an accurate response. The model uses its understanding of the question, its knowledge base, and its reasoning abilities to derive a response that directly answers the question.

The input data can take various forms depending on the complexity of the task. It can include numerical data, textual data, or even multimedia inputs like images or audio. The prompt engineer must ensure that the input data is well-prepared, properly formatted, and aligned with the expectations of the AI model being used.

In addition to the main input data, it is often helpful to provide any necessary supporting or accompanying information. This includes any relevant context, background details, or examples that can aid the model in generating more accurate and relevant responses. By carefully selecting and preparing the input data, the prompt engineer can shape the model's understanding of the task and guide it towards generating desired outputs.

It is important to note that the quality and relevance of the input data greatly influence the model's performance. The prompt engineer must ensure that the input data is representative of the overall task and provides the necessary information for the model to generate meaningful responses.

Input data forms the core of the prompt and serves as the material that the AI model processes to generate responses. It can take various forms and must be carefully selected and prepared to ensure accurate and meaningful outputs. By providing appropriate input data, prompt engineers enable the model to leverage its capabilities and produce responses that align with the desired goals of the task.

Output indicators

Output indicators play a pivotal role in prompt engineering by providing explicit instructions to the AI model regarding the desired format or structure of its response. By specifying the output indicators, prompt engineers can guide the model in generating outputs that are aligned with the expected format, making them more coherent, structured, and relevant to the specific task at hand.

The choice of output indicators depends on the nature of the task and the desired outcome. For example, if the prompt requires generating a list of items, specifying the output indicator as a list format informs the model to structure its response accordingly, itemizing each element distinctly. This helps organize the generated information into a more digestible and accessible format for the end-user.

Alternatively, if the prompt calls for a cohesive paragraph, the output indicator can be specified accordingly. In such cases, the AI model crafts a response that presents a comprehensive and unified explanation or argument, suitable for use in a document or an article.

Furthermore, output indicators can also guide the length or the complexity of the response. By specifying the desired output length, such as a single sentence or a short paragraph, the prompt engineer can control the level of detail and conciseness in the model's generated responses.

Output indicators can also assist in defining the structure of the response. For instance, if the prompt requires the model to generate a dialogue or a narrative, the output indicators can be used to instruct the model in a conversational or storytelling style. This helps the model in tailoring its responses to fit the desired mode of communication.

By providing clear and specific output indicators, prompt engineers enable the model to understand the intended format of its response and generate outputs that meet those expectations. This helps streamline the communication between the AI model and the end-user, as the generated responses are more easily consumable and meet the requirements of the task.

It is important to note that output indicators should be carefully chosen to ensure they align with the objective of the prompt and the preferences or constraints of the user. By striking the right balance and providing appropriate output indicators, prompt engineers can guide AI models to produce more precise, relevant, and usable responses.

While not every prompt requires all these elements, a well-crafted prompt often incorporates a combination of these components tailored to the specific task at hand. Each element contributes to shaping the model's output and assists in generating responses that align with the desired outcome.

Tips for Effective Prompt Design

Designing prompts for large language models (LLMs) requires understanding and manipulating specific settings that guide the model's output. Two key settings to consider are 'Temperature' and 'Top_p'.

The 'Temperature' parameter controls the randomness of the model's output. Lower values increase determinism, useful for fact-based questions. Higher values add randomness, beneficial for creative tasks like poetry generation.

The 'Top_p' parameter, used in nucleus sampling, also affects determinism. Lower values produce precise answers, while higher values increase response diversity.

Adjust either 'Temperature' or 'Top_p' individually to avoid complexity and better control the output.

Remember the importance of prompt variation depending on the LLM version you are using. Experiment with settings and prompt design to optimize results.

Key Strategies for Successful Prompt Design

1. Begin with simple prompts and gradually add complexity for enhanced results:

Starting with simple prompts is a smart strategy to get started in the prompt design process. Simple prompts help you understand the basic functionality of the language model and how it responds to different inputs. As you gain familiarity with the system and its capabilities, you can gradually increase the complexity of your prompts. By doing so, you can explore the full potential of the model and extract more intricate and nuanced responses. It's important to maintain different versions of your prompts throughout this progression so that you can compare the outputs and fine-tune your design approach. This iterative process allows you to refine your prompts and achieve better outcomes over time.

2. Break down complex tasks into simpler subtasks to prevent overwhelming the prompt design process:

When faced with complex tasks that involve multiple subtasks or require the model to perform intricate operations, it can be overwhelming to design a single prompt that encompasses everything. In such cases, it is advisable to break down the complex task into simpler subtasks. By dissecting the main task into smaller, more manageable components, you can design prompts that address each subtask separately. This not only makes the prompt design process more organized but also allows you to focus on specific aspects of the task, making it easier to elicit accurate and relevant responses from the model. Breaking down complex tasks into simpler subtasks also helps you maintain clarity and avoid information overload for the language model, ensuring that it can effectively generate outputs for each subtask.

By following these key strategies, you can enhance your prompt design process and achieve better outcomes from the language model. Starting with simple prompts and gradually increasing complexity helps you explore the model's capabilities, while breaking down complex tasks into subtasks ensures a more organized and effective prompt design approach.

Crafting Effective Prompts: The Power of Instructions

Instructions play a crucial role in prompt design as they provide guidance to the language model on the desired task execution. The choice of instructions can greatly influence the output generated by the model. By using clear and explicit instructions, prompt designers can effectively direct the model's behavior and tailor it to their specific use case.

To harness the power of instructions, it is recommended to experiment with different instruction patterns, keywords, and contexts. By testing various combinations, you can identify the most optimal instruction formulation that yields the desired outcomes. For example, you can explore different ways to instruct the model to write a story, such as "Compose a narrative about..." or "Create a fictional account of...". By testing and iterating with different instruction patterns, you can find the formulation that elicits the most suitable responses from the language model.

Instructions should be specific and relevant to your task. The more precise the instruction, the better aligned the model's output will be with your expectations. It is essential to provide clear and unambiguous instructions so that the model understands the task at hand accurately. Including specific information like the format, output length, or any specific requirements further assists in guiding the model towards generating the desired response.

To ensure clarity and separation between the instruction and the remaining prompt context, it is recommended to place the instruction at the start of the prompt. By doing so, you establish a clear boundary that distinguishes the instruction from the subsequent context. This separation helps the model comprehend the desired task more effectively and reduces any confusion that might arise due to overlapping instruction and contextual information.

A common practice is to use clear separators like "###" to demarcate the instruction section from the prompt context. This visually distinguishes the instruction, making it easier for the model to identify and follow. For instance:

"### Instruction ### Create a persuasive essay discussing the benefits of renewable energy sources."

By following these recommendations, prompt designers can harness the power of instructions to shape the language model's output to match their specific requirements. Experimenting with different instruction patterns, making instructions specific, and using clear separators ensures clarity and enhances the effectiveness of prompts in guiding the model's behavior.

The Essence of Specificity in Prompt Design

Specificity is a key factor in prompt design as it ensures that the language model understands the task accurately and produces the desired output. When crafting prompts, it is essential to provide clear and precise instructions that leave no room for ambiguity. By accurately defining the task and instruction, you can align the outcomes with your expectations more effectively.

To achieve specificity in prompt design, it can be helpful to include examples within your prompts. Examples serve as guiding references for the model, showing it the desired output format or structure. For instance, if you want the model to summarize a text into three sentences, your prompt can include an example like "Summarize the following text into three sentences: ...", providing a clear expectation of the desired output length and format. Including examples helps the model understand the desired output more accurately and increases the chances of generating responses that meet your requirements.

While specificity is important, it's also crucial to balance the length and relevance of details within the prompt. Overloading the prompt with excessive and irrelevant information can confuse the language model and hinder its ability to generate accurate responses. It's important to include only those details that meaningfully contribute to the task at hand. Keep the prompt concise, precise, and focused on the specific elements necessary for the task's successful completion.

To optimize prompt design, constant experimentation and iteration are necessary. Prompt designers should strive to refine and enhance their prompts through ongoing testing and analysis. This iterative approach allows for fine-tuning and improvement of prompts over time. By experimenting with different variations, adjusting instructions and examples, and analyzing the outputs, prompt designers can refine their prompts for optimal outcomes. This iterative process helps in understanding the language model's behavior better and finding the most effective prompts that consistently yield desired results.

Specificity is crucial in prompt design to ensure accurate understanding and alignment with your expectations. Including examples within prompts provides guidance to the language model on the desired output format. Balancing prompt length and relevance of details avoids confusion and aids the model in producing accurate responses. Constant experimentation and iteration are essential for refining prompts and optimizing outcomes. By following these principles, prompt designers can increase the effectiveness of their prompts and maximize the language model's performance.

Sidestepping Ambiguity in Prompt Design

In the realm of prompt design, it is crucial to avoid ambiguity and impreciseness. Ambiguous prompts can lead to undesirable or unexpected outputs from the language model, resulting in confusion and frustration. Clear and precise instructions are key to ensuring effective communication with the model and yielding accurate and desired results.

To avoid ambiguity, it is important to choose precise and direct instructions when crafting prompts. The language model needs explicit guidance on the task at hand, leaving no room for misinterpretation. By providing clear and specific instructions, the model can better understand the desired output and generate responses that align with your expectations. For example, instead of using vague instructions like "Discuss this topic broadly," it is more effective to provide specific direction such as "Analyze the pros and cons of this topic from an economic perspective."

Convolution and complexity in prompts should also be avoided. Intricate and convoluted prompts can confuse the model and lead to outputs that do not meet the desired criteria. It is essential to keep the prompts straightforward and focused on specific requests. By simplifying the prompt and avoiding unnecessary complexity, you can guide the model more effectively and increase the likelihood of obtaining accurate and relevant responses. Clarity in prompt design enhances the model's comprehension and ensures that it generates outputs that are aligned with your intended goals.

Striving for specificity and clarity in prompt design helps to sidestep ambiguity by providing the language model with concise and unambiguous instructions. The clearer the communication, the better the model can understand the task and generate appropriate responses. By avoiding convoluted prompts and favoring specific requests, prompt designers create a framework that guides the model effectively, enabling it to produce outputs that are more precise, relevant, and in line with the intended purpose of the task.

Sidestepping ambiguity in prompt design is therefore crucial for achieving the desired results from the language model. By choosing precise and direct instructions, avoiding convoluted prompts, and favoring specificity, prompt designers can ensure clear communication, alleviate confusion, and guide the model efficiently towards generating accurate and relevant responses.

Choosing Clarity over Restrictions

When it comes to prompt design, it is often more beneficial to instruct the language model on what to do rather than dictating what not to do. This approach emphasizes clarity and precision, ensuring that the model understands your expectations and produces the desired output. By focusing on guiding the model towards desired actions, prompt designers can maximize the effectiveness and efficiency of their prompts.

Instructing the model on what to do provides a clear framework and goal for the language model to work towards. This clarity helps to establish a shared understanding between the prompt designer and the model, reducing the chances of misinterpretation or generating irrelevant responses. For example, instead of saying "Do not include personal opinions," it is more effective to provide a positive instruction like "Provide an objective analysis based on available data."

By emphasizing the desired actions in the prompt, prompt designers can drive the model's attention towards the specific task at hand. This focused approach helps reduce the chances of the model generating outputs that do not align with the intended purpose of the prompt. Instead of spending cognitive resources on understanding and avoiding prohibited actions, the model can concentrate on executing the requested task accurately and efficiently.

Clarity and precision in prompt design are essential to ensure that the model comprehends the desired task correctly. Language models are highly sensitive to the input they receive, so using unambiguous language and concise instructions helps minimize confusion. By being specific about the desired output, output format, or any other relevant details, prompt designers can guide the model more effectively and increase the chances of obtaining the desired response.

By following the strategy of choosing clarity over restrictions, prompt designers can design effective prompts that yield the desired outputs from the language model. Instructing the model on what to do, focusing on clarity and precision, and guiding the model towards the desired actions means prompt designers establish effective communication with the model and maximize the chances of obtaining accurate and relevant responses.

Overall, prompt designers should prioritize clarity and precision in their instructions, guiding the language model towards the desired actions to ensure successful prompt design. By emphasizing what the model should do instead of what it shouldn't do, they create a clear and concise framework for the model to follow, enabling effective communication and promoting the generation of desired outputs.

Best Practices for Prompt Engineering

Craft Precise and Explicit Instructions

When crafting prompts, it is crucial – as we have emphasized above – to provide precise and explicit instructions to guide the model effectively. One effective strategy is to utilize delimiters such as commas, quotation marks, angle brackets, or HTML tags to distinguish different sections of the input. By employing these delimiters, you can structure your prompt more effectively and minimize prompt errors.

For example, if you want the model to summarize a specific text, you can use delimiters to specify the portion that needs to be summarized. By enclosing the text within appropriate delimiters, you provide clear guidance to the model on the specific task it needs to perform.

Using delimiters in this manner helps to highlight the desired input and ensures that the model understands the intended focus of the prompt. It establishes a clear boundary for the model to identify and interpret the relevant information. This can be particularly helpful when dealing with longer or more complex prompts, as it allows the model to comprehend the specific requirements and respond accordingly.

Here are specific examples of using delimiters to distinguish different sections of the input:

1. Using inverted commas as delimiters:

- Input: "Please summarize the following text: 'Lorem ipsum dolor sit amet, consectetur adipiscing elit, sed do eiusmod tempor incididunt ut labore et dolore magna aliqua.'"

- The inverted comma delimiter separates the prompt instruction from the specific text to be summarized.

2. Using quotation marks as delimiters:

- Input: "Summarize the following paragraph: "Lorem ipsum dolor sit amet, consectetur adipiscing elit. Nulla facilisi.""

- The quotation marks indicate the text that needs to be summarized, clearly distinguishing it from the prompt instruction.

3. Using angle brackets as delimiters:

- Input: "<summary> Summarize the following article: 'Lorem ipsum dolor sit amet, consectetur adipiscing elit...' </summary>"

- The angle brackets encapsulate the specific section of the input that indicates the text to be summarized.

4. Using HTML tags as delimiters:

- Input: "<p> Please summarize the following content: </p> <article> 'Lorem ipsum dolor sit amet, consectetur adipiscing elit...' </article>"

- The opening and closing HTML tags "<article></article>" demarcate the portion that contains the text to be summarized.

In each of these examples, the delimiters effectively separate the different sections of the input. This ensures that the model can identify and differentiate the prompt instruction from the specific content that needs to be processed or focused on. Using delimiters in this way enhances the structure of the input and minimizes potential prompt errors.

By using delimiters effectively, you can enhance the precision and clarity of your instructions, enabling the model to generate more accurate and contextually appropriate responses. It helps to create a structured and well-defined prompt that guides the model towards the desired outcome.

Request Structured Output

When interacting with AI models, it is often advantageous to request output in a structured format to facilitate efficient processing and manipulation. One popular and highly versatile format for structured data is JSON (JavaScript Object Notation).

By asking for the output in a JSON format, you enable the AI model to provide its responses in a structured and organized manner. JSON is a lightweight data interchange format that is widely supported by various programming languages, including Python. It allows for the representation of complex data structures using a simple and readable syntax.

One of the main advantages of using JSON is its compatibility with Python's built-in data structures, such as lists and dictionaries. JSON objects can be easily converted into equivalent Python objects, enabling seamless integration of the output into your Python codebase. This conversion process is effortless and can be done using the `json` module provided in the Python standard library.

By converting the JSON output into Python objects, you gain the ability to access and manipulate the data using the rich set of built-in methods and functions available in Python. This allows you to extract specific values, filter data based on certain criteria, or perform complex operations on the generated output.

Furthermore, JSON's flexibility and support for nested structures make it suitable for representing a wide range of data types and formats. You can easily include arrays, strings, numbers, Booleans, and even nested objects within the JSON structure. This flexibility enables you to capture and convey complex information from the AI model's output effectively.

In addition, JSON's human-readable format makes it easy to understand and work with, both for developers and other stakeholders. The clear and concise syntax of JSON helps ensure the output is easily interpretable and can be shared across different systems without loss of information or confusion.

Overall, by requesting structured output in JSON format, you create a seamless and standardized way to communicate and process the responses from AI models in your Python code. This facilitates efficient handling and manipulation of the generated output, opening up a wide range of possibilities for further analysis, visualization, or integration into larger software systems.

Verify Conditions

When crafting prompts for AI models, it is important to verify if certain conditions are met, particularly when dealing with edge cases or potential pitfalls. This helps ensure that the model responds appropriately and avoids generating inaccurate or irrelevant outputs. One effective strategy is to design the prompt in a way that verifies specific conditions before proceeding with the task.

For instance, when working with prompts that involve instructions or steps, it is crucial to confirm the presence of these instructions in the input text. To address the scenario where no steps are provided, you can instruct the model to generate a specific response such as "No steps provided" or a similar message. By explicitly prompting the model to handle this situation, you ensure that it doesn't attempt to generate instructions or outputs based on incomplete or ambiguous input.

In cases where inputs may be missing key information or include incomplete data, it is essential to guide the model to take appropriate action. By incorporating checks and validations within the prompt, you instruct the model to assess the input and respond accordingly. This approach helps prevent misleading or incorrect outputs that may result from incomplete or insufficient information.

In addition to verifying conditions, it is beneficial to guide the model through well-defined steps for handling edge cases. You can explicitly instruct the model on how to handle exceptions, undefined behaviors, or unexpected situations that may arise during the task. This ensures that the model follows a predetermined behavior and provides coherent outputs even in challenging or unconventional scenarios.

When designing prompts that confirm conditions, it is essential to provide clear and explicit instructions to the model. By setting up specific checks and validations, you create a robust prompt that guides the model in understanding and processing the input correctly. This approach enhances the reliability and accuracy of the model's responses, enabling it to handle edge cases effectively.

By verifying conditions within the prompt, you establish a stronger framework for the AI model to operate within, ensuring more reliable and contextually appropriate outputs. It enables the model to adapt to different scenarios and handle potential pitfalls, ultimately enhancing the overall performance and usefulness of the AI system.

Utilize Few-shot Prompting

When working with AI models, leveraging few-shot prompting techniques can be highly effective in enabling them to perform new tasks or generate accurate responses with limited training examples. Few-shot prompting involves providing the model with a set of successful examples of completed tasks and asking it to perform a similar task based on that limited knowledge.

By providing successful examples, you give the model a reference point and demonstrate the desired output or behavior. These examples serve as a guide for the model to generalize and learn from, even when the number of training instances is limited.

The first step in utilizing few-shot prompting is to gather a representative set of completed tasks that showcase the desired outcome. These tasks can be collected from various sources, such as human-generated examples, existing datasets, or previous model outputs that align with the task at hand.

Once you have a set of successful examples, you can present them to the model as input during fine-tuning or inference. You instruct the model to use the provided examples to understand the underlying pattern, structure, or reasoning required to carry out similar tasks. By demonstrating a range of successful outputs, you enable the model to learn and generalize from these examples, improving its ability to handle similar tasks in the future.

Using few-shot prompting techniques, you empower the model to reason and extrapolate based on the limited examples provided. This approach helps the model to transfer knowledge from the existing examples and apply it to new tasks or scenarios.

However, it's important to note that while few-shot prompting can be a powerful technique, the efficacy can vary depending on the complexity and similarity of the tasks. Models may struggle with tasks that deviate significantly from the provided few-shot examples or when faced with novel challenges that haven't been explicitly demonstrated.

To enhance the effectiveness of few-shot prompting, it is therefore essential to carefully select and curate the examples to ensure they represent a diverse range of scenarios and cover relevant variations. It's also beneficial to evaluate the model's performance on a separate set of validation examples to assess its ability to generalize beyond the few-shot examples.

By utilizing few-shot prompting, you provide the model with a foundation of successful examples to learn from, improving its capability to generalize and perform similar tasks accurately. It enables the model to leverage limited training data and adapt to new challenges, enhancing its versatility and competence in handling a wide range of tasks.

Allow the model time to process

Allowing the model sufficient time to process complex tasks is essential to ensure accurate and comprehensive outputs. To maximize the model's understanding and reasoning capabilities, it is beneficial to provide detailed steps and instructions that guide the model through a logical sequence or chain of reasoning.

For complex tasks, breaking them down into smaller, more manageable steps can help the model navigate and comprehend the task more effectively. Similar to how humans often benefit from step-by-step instructions, guiding the model through a systematic process promotes clarity, reduces ambiguity, and enhances the model's ability to generate coherent and contextually appropriate responses.

By structuring the prompt with detailed steps, you provide a roadmap for the model to follow, ensuring that it considers all relevant factors and incorporates a logical flow of information. Each step builds upon the previous ones, allowing the model to analyze the inputs, perform intermediate calculations or reasoning, and gradually progress towards generating the final output.

In addition to providing detailed steps, it is important to instruct the model to thoroughly process the task before delivering the final output. This ensures that the model takes the time to consider all relevant information, perform any necessary computations, and engage in a comprehensive analysis to generate well-grounded responses.

By instructing the model to thoroughly process the task, you emphasize the importance of thoughtful reasoning and reduce the likelihood of generating rushed or incomplete outputs. This approach encourages the model to apply critical thinking, logical reasoning, and relevant context to arrive at the most accurate and appropriate response.

Allowing the model sufficient time to process complex tasks also benefits its overall comprehension and learning. It gives the model an opportunity to explore different possibilities, consider various perspectives, and integrate relevant knowledge to provide more comprehensive and insightful outputs.

However, it's important to strike a balance between giving the model enough time for reasoning and not causing unnecessary delays. The time allotted for processing should be reasonable and aligned with the complexity of the task. Striking this balance ensures both accuracy and efficiency in generating responses.

By providing detailed steps and emphasizing thorough processing, you enable the model to navigate complex tasks more effectively. This approach promotes clarity, reduces ambiguity, and enhances the model's ability to reason logically and generate accurate outputs. Allowing the model sufficient time to process complex tasks fosters comprehension, fosters more comprehensive responses, and facilitates ongoing learning and improvement.

Opt for the latest model

When it comes to prompt engineering and working with AI models, opting for the latest and most advanced models can significantly enhance the quality and performance of the generated outputs. Choosing the latest models ensures that you have access to the most up-to-date advancements, improvements, and refinements in the field of artificial intelligence.

Using the latest models provides several benefits. Firstly, newer models often showcase enhanced capabilities in terms of understanding context, generating more accurate responses, and handling complex tasks. These advancements are a result of ongoing research and development efforts by the AI community, resulting in models that have been fine-tuned and trained on larger, more diverse datasets.

Secondly, the latest models often incorporate improvements in model architecture or training methodologies that address previous limitations or shortcomings. These enhancements can lead to improved performance, better handling of edge cases, and increased overall reliability.

Additionally, more recent models tend to leverage larger pre-training datasets. With access to larger amounts of diverse and high-quality data, these models can effectively capture a wide range of language patterns, semantic nuances, and domain-specific knowledge.

Furthermore, newer models may have benefited from ongoing evaluation and fine-tuning processes, resulting in improved performance on various benchmarks and metrics. These evaluations help refine the models and better align them with specific application requirements or user expectations.

It is worth noting that while the latest models often provide significant enhancements, their adoption also requires you to bear in mind factors such as computational resources, infrastructure requirements, and deployment considerations. It is important to assess whether the added benefits from utilizing the latest models outweigh the associated costs and considerations for your specific use case.

Staying informed about advancements in the field of AI and being aware of the latest models is crucial for prompt engineering. Regularly reviewing model releases and updates from reputable sources, research papers, or AI community forums can help you keep up to date with emerging advancements and make informed decisions regarding the selection of models for your specific tasks. Opt in to AI News at AIArchitects.ai to get the latest news on AI every week.

By opting for the latest models, you can leverage the cutting-edge advancements in AI and maximize the quality and effectiveness of the generated outputs. This approach ensures that you are benefiting from the most advanced techniques and methodologies available, ultimately enhancing the performance and value of your AI-based applications or systems.

Provide detailed descriptions

When crafting prompts, it's crucial to provide detailed descriptions to guide AI models effectively and ensure accurate and contextually appropriate responses. Being specific and descriptive about various aspects such as the required context, outcome, length, format, style, and more helps to set clear expectations and optimize the generated outputs.

Context is particularly important as it establishes the background information necessary for the model to understand and generate relevant responses. Clearly specifying the context helps the model narrow down its focus and ensures that it generates responses that are appropriate within the given context.

Additionally, describing the desired outcome provides the model with a clear target or goal to work towards. This helps align the model's understanding of what needs to be achieved, enabling it to generate outputs that are in line with the intended objective.

Including details about the desired length of the response is essential for controlling the level of detail and succinctness. For instance, you can specify whether you need a brief summary, a comprehensive essay, or a specific word count. This prevents the model from providing unnecessarily lengthy or overly concise responses, ensuring that the generated output meets the desired length requirements.

In some cases, specifying the desired format or style can also be beneficial. For example, if you are asking the model to generate code, it is useful to indicate the programming language or provide any specific conventions to follow. Providing guidance on the format or style ensures that the model generates outputs that align with the preferred guidelines or standards.

When describing these various aspects, it is important to be as specific and explicit as possible. Avoid vague or ambiguous instructions that could lead to misinterpretation or incorrect outputs. By providing precise and detailed descriptions, you reduce any potential confusion or ambiguity surrounding the task at hand, facilitating the model's understanding and improving the accuracy of the generated responses.

Furthermore, incorporating relevant examples or illustrations can greatly enhance the prompt. By demonstrating the desired format, style, or outcome through examples, you provide the model with concrete references to follow. This approach simplifies the understanding and interpretation of the prompt requirements and can help the model generate outputs that closely match the desired format or style.

Overall, providing detailed descriptions in your prompts ensures that AI models have clear guidance and expectations for generating accurate and contextually appropriate responses. Being specific about the required context, outcome, length, format, style, and other relevant aspects helps optimize the models' understanding and performance, and results in more precise and tailored outputs that align with your specific requirements.

Applications of Prompt Engineering

Program-aided Language Model (PAL)

Program-aided language models in prompt engineering involve integrating programmatic instructions and structures to enhance the capabilities of language models. By incorporating additional programming logic and constraints, PAL enables more precise and context-aware responses. This approach allows developers to guide the model's behavior, specify the desired output format, provide relevant examples, and refine prompts based on intermediate results. With the help of programmatic guidance, PAL techniques empower language models to generate accurate and tailored responses. This makes them valuable tools for a wide range of applications in natural language processing.

For example, consider the prompt:

Prompt:

Given a list of numbers, compute the sum of all even numbers.

Input: [2, 5, 8, 10, 3, 6]

Output: The sum of all even numbers is 26.

Here, the prompt includes a programmatic instruction to compute the sum of even numbers in a given list. By providing this specific task and format, the language model guided by PAL techniques can generate a response that precisely fulfills the desired computation. The integration of programmatic logic and instructions in the prompt ensures accurate and contextually appropriate results.

Generating Data

Generating data is an essential application of prompt engineering, particularly when working with large language models (LLMs). LLMs have the ability to generate coherent and contextually relevant text, which can be leveraged to create synthetic data for various purposes.

For instance, in natural language processing tasks, generating data using LLMs can be valuable for training and evaluating models. By designing prompts that instruct the LLM to generate specific types of data, such as question-answer pairs, text summaries, or dialogue interactions, researchers and practitioners can create large volumes of labeled training data. This synthetic data can then be used to train and improve NLP models, as well as to evaluate their performance.

Consider the example prompt:

Prompt:

Generate 100 question-answer pairs about famous landmarks.

Using this prompt, the LLM can generate a diverse set of question-answer pairs related to famous landmarks around the world. The generated data can be used to enhance question-answering models or to augment existing datasets for training and evaluation.

By employing prompt engineering techniques, researchers and developers can effectively utilize LLMs to generate data that aligns with their specific needs. This enables them to conduct experiments, evaluate models, and advance various domains of research.

Generating Code

Another valuable application of prompt engineering is generating code using large language models. LLMs can be prompted to generate code snippets, functions, or even entire programs, which can be beneficial in software development, automation, and programming education.

Let's consider an example where a developer wants to generate a Python function that calculates the factorial of a number:

Prompt:

Write a Python function named "factorial" that takes an integer as input and returns its factorial.

By providing this specific prompt to the LLM, it can generate code that implements the factorial function in Python:

Generated Code:

```
def factorial(n):

if n == 0 or n == 1:

return 1

else:

return n * factorial(n - 1)
```

The generated code demonstrates the recursive implementation of the factorial function in Python.

Prompt engineering allows developers to design prompts with clear instructions and specifications, such as function names, input requirements, and desired output formats. By carefully crafting prompts, LLMs can be guided to generate code snippets tailored to specific programming tasks or requirements.

This application of prompt engineering can be highly beneficial for developers seeking assistance in code generation, automating repetitive tasks, or even for educational purposes where learners can explore different code patterns and learn from the generated examples.

Risks Associated with Prompting and Solutions

As we delve into the vast potential of large language models (LLMs) and explore their capabilities, it is essential to acknowledge and address the risks and potential misuses associated with prompting. While well-crafted prompts can yield impressive results, it is crucial to understand the potential pitfalls and safety considerations when using LLMs for real-world applications. By fully recognizing and mitigating these risks, we can ensure the responsible and ethical utilization of these powerful language models.

Adversarial Prompting

Adversarial prompting involves intentionally manipulating prompts to exploit vulnerabilities or biases in language models, resulting in unintended or harmful outputs. Various techniques are employed in adversarial prompting, such as prompt injection, prompt leaking, and jailbreaking:

- Prompt Injection: This technique involves inserting additional instructions or content into the prompt to influence the model's behavior. By injecting specific keywords, phrases, or instructions, the model's output can be manipulated to produce desired or undesired outcomes. Prompt injection can introduce biases, generate offensive or harmful content, or manipulate the model's understanding of the task.

- Prompt Leaking: Prompt leaking occurs when sensitive or confidential information unintentionally gets exposed in the model's response. This can happen when the model incorporates parts of the prompt, including personally identifiable information, into its generated output. Prompt leaking poses privacy and security risks, as it may disclose sensitive data to unintended recipients or expose vulnerabilities in the model's handling of input prompts.

- Jailbreaking: Jailbreaking involves bypassing or overriding safety mechanisms put in place to regulate the behavior of language models. It entails manipulating the prompt in a way that allows the model to generate outputs that may be inappropriate, unethical, or against the intended guidelines. Jailbreaking can lead to the generation of offensive content, misinformation, or other undesirable outcomes.

To combat adversarial prompting, responsible prompt engineering practices should be adopted:

- Explicit Instructions: Emphasize the desired behavior explicitly in the instruction given to the model. While not foolproof, this approach highlights the power of well-crafted prompts in guiding the model towards the intended output.

- Parameterizing Prompt Components: Separate instructions from inputs by parameterizing different components of the prompt. Treating instructions and inputs differently can lead to cleaner and safer solutions, albeit with some trade-offs in flexibility.

- Quotes and Additional Formatting: Escaping or quoting input strings can prevent certain prompt injections. This tactic, helps maintain robustness across phrasing variations and emphasizes the importance of proper formatting and careful consideration of prompt structure.

- Adversarial Prompt Detector: Leverage language models themselves to detect and filter out adversarial prompts. By fine-tuning or training an LLM specifically for detecting such prompts, an additional layer of defense can be incorporated to mitigate the impact of adversarial inputs.

- Selecting Model Types: Choosing the appropriate model type can contribute to defense against prompt injections. Utilizing fine-tuned models or creating k-shot prompts for non-instruct models can be effective for certain tasks. Fine-tuning a model on a large number of examples can improve robustness and accuracy, reducing reliance on instruction-based models.

- Guardrails and Safety Measures: Some language models incorporate guardrails and safety measures to prevent malicious or dangerous prompts. While offering protection to a certain extent, these measures are not perfect and can still be susceptible to novel adversarial prompts. Recognizing the trade-off between safety constraints and desired behaviors is important.

Factuality

Factuality is a crucial risk in prompting, as LLMs can generate responses that appear coherent and convincing but may lack accuracy. To address this risk, several solutions can be employed:

- Provide Ground Truth: Incorporate reliable and factual information as part of the context to guide the model in generating more accurate responses. This can involve referencing related articles, excerpts from reputable sources, or specific sections from Wikipedia entries. By incorporating verified information, the model is less likely to produce fabricated or inconsistent responses.

- Control Response Diversity: Modifying the probability parameters of the model can influence the diversity of its responses. By decreasing the probability values, the model can be guided towards generating more focused and factually accurate answers. Additionally, explicitly instructing the model to acknowledge uncertainty by admitting when it doesn't possess the required knowledge can mitigate the risk of generating false information.

- Provide Examples in the Prompt: Including a combination of questions and responses in the prompt can guide the model to differentiate between topics it is familiar with and those it is not. By explicitly demonstrating examples of both known and unknown information, the model can better understand the boundaries of its knowledge and avoid generating false or speculative responses.

These solutions help address the risk of factuality in prompting by promoting more accurate and reliable output from LLMs. It is crucial to continuously evaluate and refine prompt engineering strategies to strike the right balance between generating coherent responses and maintaining factual accuracy.

Biases

Biases in LLMs pose a substantial risk, as they can lead to the generation of problematic and biased content. Biases can negatively impact the performance of the model in downstream tasks and perpetuate harmful stereotypes or discriminatory behavior. To address this risk, it is vital to implement appropriate solutions:

- Effective Prompting Strategies: Craft well-designed prompts that encourage fairness and inclusivity to mitigate biases. Providing specific instructions and context can guide the model to generate more unbiased responses. Incorporating diverse and representative examples in the prompt helps the model learn from a broader range of perspectives, reducing the likelihood of biased output.

- Moderation and Filtering: Implement robust moderation and filtering mechanisms to identify and mitigate biased content generated by LLMs. Develop systems capable of detecting and flagging potentially biased or harmful outputs in real-time. Human reviewers or content moderation teams can review and address any problematic content, ensuring that biased or discriminatory responses are not propagated.

- Diverse Training Data: Train LLMs on diverse datasets that encompass a wide range of perspectives and experiences. Exposing the model to a more comprehensive set of examples helps it learn to generate responses that are more balanced and representative. Regularly updating and expanding the training data with diverse sources further enhances the model's ability to generate unbiased content.

- Post-processing and Debiasing Techniques: Apply post-processing techniques to the generated output to identify and mitigate biases. Analyze the model's responses for potential biases and adjust them to ensure fairness and inclusivity. Debiasing methods can be employed to retrain the model, explicitly addressing and reducing biases in its output.

It is important to note that addressing biases in LLMs is an ongoing challenge, and no single solution can completely eliminate biases. It requires a combination of thoughtful prompt engineering, robust moderation practices, diverse training data, and continuous improvement of the underlying models. Close collaboration between researchers, practitioners, and communities is crucial to develop effective strategies and ensure responsible and unbiased use of LLMs

Conclusion

In conclusion, prompt engineering stands as a critical pillar in the future of language model learning. Its significance lies in its ability to bridge the gap between AI and human language, enabling effective and intuitive communication. As we witness the ongoing evolution of prompt engineering, its potential becomes increasingly apparent.

Within the realm of large language models, well-crafted prompts serve as a guiding force, steering machine learning models through the complexities of human language with precision and comprehension. As AI technologies become further integrated into our lives – in the form of driverless cars, voice assistants, AI chatbots, and more – the role of prompt engineering in creating context-aware prompts becomes even more vital.

Looking ahead, prompt engineering will play a central role in emerging fields like automated content creation, data analysis, and healthcare diagnostics. It goes beyond merely formulating questions for AI responses; it involves understanding the context, intent, and desired outcomes and encapsulating them within concise and effective prompts.

Investing in prompt engineering today will have far-reaching implications for our AI-enabled future. It will fuel advancements in large language models and lay the foundation for unimaginable AI technologies yet to come. Skilled prompt engineers hold the key to unlocking the potential of LLMs and shaping the AI-integrated world that lies ahead of us. As we embark on this transformative journey, the future of language model learning rests firmly in their hands.

Prompt engineering is both a science and an art, involving meticulous detail orientation and a splash of creativity. The above-mentioned techniques create a foundation for crafting effective and tailored prompts, but the wonderful world of AI offers much room for exploration and innovation. Happy engineering!

Transforming Knowledge Work with GPT Technology

In today's rapidly evolving world, knowledge workers play a vital role in driving innovation, problem-solving, and critical decision-making within organizations. These professionals rely heavily on their cognitive abilities and access to extensive information sources to perform their duties effectively. However, as the volume of information continues to grow exponentially, managing and making sense of it all can become overwhelming.

Luckily, with the advancements in Generative Pre-trained Transformer (GPT) technology, knowledge workers now have an incredible tool at their disposal. GPT-powered applications can enhance productivity, automate repetitive tasks, and augment decision-making capabilities across various organizational departments. In this chapter, we will delve into how GPT technology can revolutionize knowledge work across different organizational functions.

Human Resources

GPT technology is increasingly being used in HR departments to streamline and automate various workforce management processes. For instance, recruiters can leverage GPT-powered tools to create more accurate and engaging job descriptions, ensuring they attract the right talent. Companies can also employ chatbots integrated with GPT to answer frequently asked HR-related questions, reducing the burden on HR professionals while increasing response times.

Expanding on the impact of GPT technology in the Human Resources department, let's examine in more detail how it can revolutionize workforce management processes and improve overall efficiency.

Job Descriptions

Creating compelling and accurate job descriptions is crucial for attracting qualified candidates. GPT-powered tools can enhance this process by analyzing vast amounts of data and generating job descriptions that are both captivating and align closely with the required skills and qualifications. By utilizing GPT algorithms, HR professionals can save time and effort while crafting job descriptions that accurately communicate the role's expectations and attract the right talent.

Chatbots for HR Support

HR departments are often inundated with various queries from employees ranging from leave policies to benefits and company policies. GPT-powered chatbots can be incorporated into the company's intranet or HR portal to address these frequently asked questions promptly and accurately. These chatbots can understand the context of the question and provide relevant responses, freeing up HR professionals' time to focus on more complex and strategic tasks.

Employee Onboarding and Training

GPT technology can streamline the employee onboarding process by automating certain aspects, such as providing access to relevant documents, policies, and procedures. By training the GPT algorithms on the company's specific onboarding material, the chatbot can guide new hires through the process, answer routine questions, and provide necessary resources, ensuring a consistent and efficient onboarding experience.

Additionally, GPT-powered tools can contribute to employee training initiatives. By analyzing existing training materials, GPT algorithms can generate personalized training content, reinforce learning objectives, and provide real-time assistance during training sessions. This can enhance the overall effectiveness and engagement of training programs while reducing the time and effort required from HR professionals.

Performance Management

Managing and evaluating employee performance can be a time-consuming task for HR professionals. GPT technology can assist in this facet as well. By analyzing performance data, feedback, and other relevant information, GPT algorithms can provide valuable insights into employee performance, identifying patterns, trends, and areas for improvement. This data-driven approach can support HR professionals in making more informed decisions regarding promotions, rewards, and development opportunities.

Employee Engagement

Building and maintaining employee engagement is a priority for HR departments. By leveraging GPT-powered applications, HR professionals can analyze employee feedback surveys, sentiment analysis, and other data sources to gain insights into the overall employee sentiment and engagement levels within the organization. These insights can guide HR professionals in implementing targeted initiatives to improve employee satisfaction and address any areas of concern.

GPT technology in HR departments brings a multitude of benefits, contributing to improved workforce management processes and increased efficiency. By utilizing GPT-powered tools for creating accurate job descriptions, providing HR support through chatbots, enhancing onboarding and training processes, simplifying performance management, and enhancing employee engagement initiatives, HR professionals can optimize their time and focus on strategic and value-added tasks. Implementing GPT technology in HR departments empowers organizations to attract, retain, and develop the right talent while fostering a positive employee experience.

Marketing

The field of marketing heavily relies on analysizing vast amounts of data and generating creative content. By harnessing the power of GPT, marketers can automate tedious tasks and generate high-quality content efficiently. GPT algorithms can be trained to generate personalized marketing emails, social media posts, and even ad copy. Marketers can use these generated drafts as a starting point, saving valuable time and resources while ensuring consistent messaging.

Expanding on the impact of GPT technology in the marketing field, let's explore how it can revolutionize marketing processes and facilitate efficient content creation.

Content Automation

GPT-powered algorithms can alleviate the burden of content creation by automating repetitive tasks and generating high-quality content. Marketers can train the algorithms on existing marketing materials and brand guidelines, enabling them to produce personalized marketing emails, social media posts, and ad copy. Using these generated drafts as a basis, marketers can then fine-tune and customize the content to align with specific campaigns, target audiences, and brand messaging. This automation significantly reduces the time and effort required for content creation, allowing marketers to focus more on strategy and innovation.

Consistency and Branding

Maintaining consistent messaging and branding across multiple marketing channels is critical for building brand recognition and trust. GPT-powered algorithms can ensure a cohesive brand voice by generating content that aligns with established brand guidelines. Marketers can use these generated drafts as starting points, saving time and resources by starting with a solid foundation that adheres to brand standards. This consistency across various marketing materials enhances brand recognition and strengthens the overall marketing efforts.

Creativity and Idea Generation

GPT technology can also assist marketers in generating fresh and innovative ideas for campaigns. By training GPT algorithms on a wide range of marketing concepts, successful campaigns, and consumer trends, marketers can leverage them as idea-generation tools. Marketers can input prompts or topics, allowing the algorithms to generate creative campaign concepts, taglines, or content angles that may inspire new marketing strategies. These generated ideas can serve as valuable sparks for innovation and brainstorming sessions, providing marketers with a broader range of possibilities to explore.

Content Personalization

Personalization is a critical element in successful marketing campaigns. GPT technology can aid marketers in delivering personalized messages by analyzing customer data, preferences, and past behavior. Marketers can train GPT algorithms on customer profiles, purchase history, and interaction data to generate personalized content that resonates with individual customers. This level of personalization enables marketers to deliver more targeted and relevant campaigns, leading to increased customer engagement and conversion rates.

Market Research and Analysis

GPT-powered algorithms can also contribute to market research efforts by analyzing vast amounts of data and extracting valuable insights. Marketers can utilize GPT algorithms to process customer feedback, social media conversations, market trends, and competitor analysis to provide valuable information for strategic decision-making. This analysis helps marketers identify emerging trends, consumer sentiments, and competitive advantages, and enables them to optimize marketing strategies and stay ahead in the market.

GPT technology has tremendous potential to transform marketing processes and improve efficiency. By automating content creation, maintaining consistency and branding, facilitating idea generation, enabling personalized messaging, and enhancing market research capabilities, marketers can optimize their efforts, and save time and resources. Leveraging GPT-powered applications empowers them to create compelling and personalized content that resonates with their target audience to drive engagement and achieve their marketing goals. As marketers adapt to a rapidly changing landscape, GPT technology gives them a valuable tool to not only enhance creativity and improve efficiency but also deliver impactful and successful marketing campaigns.

Customer Service

With GPT technology, customer service departments can enhance their efficiency by utilizing chatbots for initial interactions and issue resolution. These intelligent bots can analyze customer queries, provide accurate responses, and even escalate complex issues to human representatives when needed. By reducing response times and handling repetitive tasks, GPT-powered customer service tools improve overall customer experience.

Expanding on the impact of GPT technology in customer service, let's explore how it can improve efficiency and enhance overall customer experience.

Automated Customer Interactions

GPT-powered chatbots have become increasingly popular in customer service departments. These intelligent bots can analyze customer queries, understand context, and provide accurate responses. By automating initial interactions, GPT-powered chatbots can handle a significant volume of routine inquiries, such as frequently asked questions or basic troubleshooting, without the need for human involvement. This automation drastically reduces response times, allowing customers to receive immediate assistance, even outside of traditional business hours.

Efficient Issue Resolution

In addition to handling routine queries, GPT-powered chatbots can assist in issue resolution. By analyzing customer complaints or technical issues, these bots can provide initial troubleshooting steps or recommend solutions based on predefined guidelines. This enables customers to find immediate resolutions to common problems without having to wait for human intervention. If a complex issue arises that requires human expertise, the chatbots can intelligently escalate the conversation to a human representative, ensuring a seamless transition and efficient problem-solving.

24/7 Availability and Support

Unlike human representatives, GPT-powered chatbots do not require sleep or breaks. This means they can provide continuous support to customers, addressing inquiries and resolving issues at any time of the day. By being available 24/7, GPT-powered chatbots ensure that customers can find assistance whenever they need it, enhancing overall customer satisfaction and loyalty.

Consistent and Accurate Responses

Customer service representatives might have variations in how they respond to customer queries. However, GPT-powered chatbots ensure consistent messaging and accurate information as they are programmed to provide responses based on predefined guidelines and access to a vast amount of knowledge. This consistency and accuracy contribute to a positive customer experience, as customers receive reliable information and a uniform service standard regardless of who they interact with.

Data Analysis for Continuous Improvement

GPT-powered customer service tools can collect and analyze customer interactions, providing valuable insights for continuous improvement. By analyzing customer feedback, chat logs, and patterns of inquiries, organizations can identify common pain points, areas for improvement, or emerging trends. This data-driven approach enables organizations to make informed decisions in optimizing their customer service processes, enhancing overall efficiency, and tailoring their products or services to better meet customer needs.

Human-Chatbot Collaboration

It is important to note that GPT-powered chatbots should not replace human representatives entirely. Instead, they should complement their work. Human agents can focus on complex or sensitive customer interactions, where empathy and judgment are critical, while the chatbots handle repetitive and routine queries. This collaboration between human agents and chatbots empowers customer service departments to allocate their resources effectively, ensuring high-quality service delivery.

GPT-powered customer service tools revolutionize the way organizations handle customer inquiries and issue resolution. By automating routine interactions, providing efficient issue resolution, offering 24/7 availability, ensuring consistent and accurate responses, and analyzing data for continuous improvement, customer service departments can enhance efficiency and elevate the overall customer experience. The integration of GPT technology allows organizations to achieve faster response times, improved customer satisfaction, and increased productivity, all while providing a seamless and personalized support experience.

Research and Development

Knowledge workers involved in research and development can also benefit greatly from GPT technology. GPT models can efficiently analyze vast amounts of scientific literature, patents, and research papers, assisting researchers in identifying relevant information quickly. This acceleration of information synthesis and retrieval empowers scientists and engineers to make swifter progress, enabling organizations to stay at the forefront of innovation.

Expanding on the impact of GPT technology in research and development (R&D), let's explore how it can enhance knowledge workers' efficiency and contribute to innovation.

Rapid Literature Review

One of the most time-consuming tasks in research is conducting literature reviews to identify relevant studies, patents, and research papers. GPT-powered algorithms can streamline this process by analyzing vast amounts of scientific literature and extracting key insights and findings. By automating the initial stages of literature review, researchers can save significant time, allowing them to focus more on analyzing and synthesizing the information gathered.

Improved Information Retrieval

GPT models excel at information retrieval, assisting researchers in quickly finding the most relevant documents and data sources. Researchers can input specific queries or topics into GPT-powered applications, enabling them to retrieve highly targeted and accurate results from a wide range of sources. This accelerates the data curation process and increases overall productivity, which allows researchers to access and utilize valuable information more efficiently.

Assistance in Data Analysis

GPT technology can also support knowledge workers in conducting data analysis tasks. Researchers can leverage GPT-powered algorithms to process and analyze complex datasets, extracting patterns, insights, and correlations that might not be immediately apparent. By automating certain stages of data analysis, GPT technology allows researchers to focus on interpreting the results and drawing meaningful conclusions. This enhances the quality and efficiency of their work.

Enhanced Idea Generation

GPT-powered applications can assist researchers in generating ideas for new research projects and innovative approaches. By training GPT algorithms on a wide range of scientific concepts and existing research, researchers can input prompts or topics to stimulate idea generation. The algorithms can generate novel research directions, hypotheses, or experimental designs – sparking innovative thinking and expanding the scope of exploration. This can lead to breakthroughs and discoveries that might have otherwise been overlooked.

Streamlined Collaboration and Knowledge Sharing

GPT technology enables improved collaboration and knowledge sharing among researchers. GPT-powered tools can analyze and categorize research data, organizing it in a structured manner for easy retrieval and sharing. This facilitates efficient collaboration across distributed teams and enables knowledge workers to access, contribute, and exchange information seamlessly. GPT-powered chatbots can also serve as virtual assistants, providing team members with real-time access to relevant information or expert knowledge, fostering a more connected and collaborative research environment.

Staying at the Forefront of Innovation

By leveraging the capabilities of GPT technology, organizations can enhance their R&D departments' efficiency, enabling them to stay at the forefront of innovation. Rapid synthesis of information, efficient data analysis, accelerated idea generation, and streamlined collaboration processes facilitated by GPT technology directly contribute to faster research progress and more impactful discoveries. This advantage allows organizations to develop novel products, technologies, and solutions that drive innovation and maintain a competitive edge in their respective industries.

GPT technology revolutionizes the way knowledge workers in research and development departments conduct their work. By expediting literature reviews, improving information retrieval, assisting in data analysis, stimulating idea generation, and facilitating collaboration and knowledge sharing, GPT-powered applications significantly enhance researchers' efficiency and contribute to innovation. Organizations that adopt GPT technology in their R&D processes create an environment conducive to faster research progress, enabling them to harness knowledge effectively and generate valuable insights that drive breakthroughs and advancements.

Legal

GPT-powered tools can revolutionize the legal sector by automating repetitive legal writing tasks. For instance, drafting legal contracts, reviewing documents for relevant clauses, or even generating initial case summaries can be accomplished faster and more accurately with GPT technology. This allows legal professionals to focus on higher-value work, such as strategizing, negotiating, and advising clients.

Expanding on the impact of GPT technology in the legal sector, let's explore how it can transform legal workflows and improve the efficiency of legal professionals.

Automated Document Drafting

Drafting legal contracts, agreements, or other legal documents requires careful attention to detail and adherence to specific legal language. GPT-powered tools can automate this process by generating initial drafts based on predefined templates and legal guidelines. Legal professionals can input specific requirements and parameters, allowing the GPT algorithms to generate accurate and customized drafts in a fraction of the time it would take to do manually. Lawyers can then simply review and refine these drafts. This leaves them free to focus their major efforts on higher-value work, such as analyzing complex legal issues or negotiating terms.

Efficient Document Review

Reviewing lengthy legal documents for relevant clauses, identifying potential risks, or searching for specific information can be time-consuming and prone to oversight. GPT-powered algorithms can assist legal professionals in analyzing documents efficiently. They can quickly review and extract relevant information, flag potential issues, and identify clauses that may require further scrutiny. By streamlining the document review process, legal professionals can devote more time to analyzing the legal implications and formulating strategic advice for their clients.

Case Summarization and Legal Research

GPT technology can greatly simplify legal research and case summarization. By training GPT algorithms on vast legal databases and precedents, legal professionals can extract key information and generate initial case summaries. This automated summarization process saves time and effort, enabling lawyers to rapidly identify relevant case law, evaluate legal arguments, and determine the strength or weakness of a case. This efficient retrieval of legal information enhances legal professionals' ability to provide accurate advice and make informed decisions.

Legal Analytics and Predictive Insights

GPT-powered tools are equipped with the ability to analyze vast amounts of legal data and extract meaningful insights. By analyzing historical case outcomes, legal professionals can leverage these insights to make informed predictions about the potential outcome of ongoing cases. Furthermore, GPT algorithms can assist legal professionals in assessing potential risks and evaluating the strength of legal arguments. This data-driven approach empowers lawyers with comprehensive analytics, enabling them to formulate strategies and advice based on quantitative analysis and predictive modeling.

Enhanced Client Communication

GPT technology also plays a role in optimizing client communication. By automating routine inquiries or providing initial responses, GPT-powered chatbots can handle client queries promptly and accurately, reducing response times and ensuring consistent messaging. This allows legal professionals to focus their attention on complex client needs, developing tailored strategies, and providing high-quality legal advice.

Improved Productivity and Time Management

The automation of repetitive legal writing tasks, efficient document review, accelerated legal research, and enhanced client communication provided by GPT technology significantly increases legal professionals' productivity. By saving time on routine and administrative tasks, legal professionals can allocate more time to strategic thinking, case analysis, negotiation, and client interactions. This improved time management and increased productivity ultimately lead to better client service and enhanced outcomes.

GPT technology revolutionizes legal workflows, freeing legal professionals from time-consuming and repetitive tasks. By automating document drafting, streamlining document review, facilitating case summarization and legal research, providing legal analytics, optimizing client communication, and improving productivity, GPT-powered tools enable legal professionals to focus on critical thinking, strategy development, and delivering high-quality legal services to their clients. The integration of GPT technology into the legal sector will empower legal professionals to work more efficiently, make well-informed decisions, and achieve better outcomes for their clients.

Accounting and Finance

The application of GPT technology extends beyond traditional knowledge work departments and can significantly benefit professionals in accounting and finance as well. Let's explore how GPT can enhance the efficiency and effectiveness of knowledge workers in these critical departments:

Automated Financial Reporting

Generating financial reports, such as balance sheets and income statements, can be time-consuming and prone to errors. GPT-powered algorithms can automate this process by analyzing financial data and generating accurate, standardized reports. This automation saves valuable time, reduces the risk of human error, and allows accounting professionals to focus on higher-value tasks, such as data analysis and strategic decision-making.

Data Analysis and Predictive Insights

GPT technology can assist accounting and finance professionals in data analysis tasks. When you train GPT algorithms on vast financial datasets, they can extract patterns, trends, and correlations that provide you with valuable insights for forecasting, budgeting, and risk assessment. This data-driven approach enables you to make informed decisions and predictions, leading to more effective financial strategies and improved outcomes.

Streamlined Auditing Processes

Auditing is a critical function in accounting departments, ensuring accuracy and compliance. GPT technology can speed up the auditing process by analyzing large volumes of financial transactions, identifying anomalies, and flagging potential risks. With this assistance, auditors can focus their efforts on investigating and resolving complex issues while relying on GPT-powered applications to handle routine audit tasks, improving overall efficiency.

Fraud Detection and Prevention

GPT-powered tools can also enhance fraud detection and prevention efforts within accounting and finance departments. By training GPT algorithms on historical fraud cases, these tools can identify suspicious patterns, anomalies, or potentially fraudulent activities. The algorithms can continuously monitor financial data, alerting professionals to potential risks promptly. This early detection plays a crucial role in preventing financial loss and protecting the organization's reputation.

Compliance and Regulation

Ensuring adherence to complex financial regulations and compliance requirements is paramount for accounting and finance professionals. GPT technology can assist in navigating these intricacies by analyzing regulatory documents and providing guidance on compliance best practices. This support helps professionals stay updated with evolving regulations, reducing compliance-related risks and facilitating the smooth operation of financial processes.

Financial Strategy and Planning

GPT-powered applications can contribute to financial strategy and planning efforts by analyzing market trends, economic indicators, and historical performance data. By leveraging GPT-generated predictive insights, accounting and finance professionals can make data-informed decisions when developing financial strategies and pursuing growth opportunities. This strategic approach enables organizations to achieve long-term financial goals and optimize resource allocation.

Incorporating GPT technology into accounting and finance departments empowers professionals to streamline processes, improve data analysis, enhance auditing practices, detect fraud, ensure compliance, and optimize financial strategy and planning. With GPT as a powerful tool, accounting and finance professionals can focus on higher-level financial analysis, strategic decision-making, and valuable contributions to driving the organization's financial success.

Conclusion

In conclusion, the use of GPT technology has the potential to revolutionize knowledge work across various organizational departments. From Human Resources to Marketing, to Customer Service, Research and Development, and Legal, GPT-powered applications can enhance productivity, automate repetitive tasks, and augment decision-making capabilities. By leveraging the power of GPT models, organizations can unlock efficiency and streamline their workflows, allowing their knowledge workers to focus on higher-value activities.

We've seen how GPT technology offers numerous benefits, including the ability to generate personalized job descriptions, answer HR-related queries through chatbots, automate content creation in marketing, enhance customer service with intelligent bots, expedite research and data analysis, and automate legal writing tasks. These efficiencies lead to faster decision-making, improved customer experience, increased productivity, and the ability to stay at the forefront of innovation.

Using Natural Language to Query Enterprise Data

In today's data-driven world, organizations are faced with the challenge of efficiently extracting insights from their vast repositories of enterprise data. Traditional methods of data querying can be complex and require technical expertise. However, there is a solution that simplifies the process and empowers users across the organization to derive valuable insights. By harnessing the power of natural language to query your enterprise data repository, you can unlock a new level of productivity, agility, and intelligence. In this chapter, we will explore the benefits of using natural language querying and how it can transform your organization's data analytics capabilities.

The Power of Natural Language Querying

Gone are the days of writing complex queries or relying solely on data analysts to extract information from your data repository. Natural language querying allows users to interact with data repositories using everyday language – just like having a conversation. By leveraging advanced natural language processing (NLP) techniques and powerful AI algorithms, organizations can enable users across various departments and roles to directly ask questions and get instant answers from their data.

Benefits for the Organization

Increased Productivity and Efficiency

By enabling natural language querying, organizations can empower business users, from the C-suite to front-line employees, to directly access the data they need. This reduces their dependency on technical teams and enables faster decision-making. Employees can simply ask questions in plain language, improving overall productivity, and streamlining workflows.

Democratization of Data

Democratization of data is a critical benefit that natural language querying brings to organizations. Traditionally, data analytics has been predominantly controlled by technical experts such as data analysts or data scientists. These experts possess the knowledge and skills required to write complex queries and extract insights from the data repository.

However, this approach creates a bottleneck in the organization's ability to leverage data for decision-making. Business users, who often have limited technical backgrounds, may find it difficult to access and understand the insights locked within the data. This lack of accessibility leads to a dependency on technical experts to provide them with the necessary analysis, causing delays in decision-making processes.

Natural language querying breaks down these barriers by allowing anyone within the organization to easily access and interact with the data repository. Business users can directly ask questions in plain language and receive instant answers. They no longer need technical experts to translate their questions into complex queries or create custom reports.

This democratization of data enables business users to tap into the power of data analytics and draw meaningful insights in real-time. It promotes a culture of data-driven decision-making throughout the organization, as users at all levels and across different departments can now independently access and interpret the data. They can quickly gather the information they need to support their decision-making processes

Faster Time-to-Insights

Faster time-to-insights is a significant advantage of leveraging natural language querying in data analytics. Traditional methods of data extraction and analysis often involve multiple steps, including formulating complex queries, waiting for technical teams to run the queries, and then interpreting the results. This process can be time-consuming and may result in delayed insights, hindering an organization's ability to respond quickly to market changes or emerging trends.

With natural language querying, users can obtain real-time answers to their questions directly from the data repository. By simply asking a question in plain language, users can quickly access the relevant data and receive instant insights. This eliminates the need for manual query writing, execution, and analysis, and dramatically reduces the time it takes to arrive at actionable insights.

The ability to access real-time information in a timely manner therefore enhances the organization's agility and responsiveness. Decision-makers can stay up-to-date with the latest data trends, make informed decisions, and act promptly to seize new opportunities. By reducing the time it takes to obtain insights, natural language querying empowers teams to be proactive rather than reactive, enabling them to stay ahead in a fast-paced and competitive environment.

Moreover, natural language querying facilitates exploratory data analysis. Users can ask ad-hoc questions and iteratively refine their inquiries in real-time.

Enhanced Collaboration and Data Exploration

Enhanced collaboration and data exploration are key benefits of adopting natural language querying in an organization's data analytics processes. Traditional methods of data analysis often involve a siloed approach, where individuals or teams work independently on their specific tasks. This siloed approach can hinder the discovery of hidden patterns and insights, as different perspectives and expertise may not be shared effectively.

Natural language querying changes this dynamic by providing a conversational interface that enables users to understand, access, and share data seamlessly. It encourages knowledge exchange and collaboration within teams, breaking down the barriers between different roles and departments. Users can easily discuss and explore data together, leveraging their unique perspectives and expertise to uncover insights that might have otherwise gone unnoticed.

Through the use of natural language, users can have collaborative conversations about the data, ask follow-up questions, and explore various angles of analysis in real-time. This iterative process allows teams to dive deep into the data, test hypotheses, and uncover hidden relationships or patterns. Importantly, by fostering collaboration around data exploration, organizations can tap into the collective intelligence of their teams and generate valuable insights that have the potential to drive innovation, identify new opportunities, and solve complex problems.

Furthermore, with the ability to easily share and communicate data insights using natural language querying, organizations can facilitate cross-functional collaboration.

Improved Data Governance and Compliance

Improved data governance and compliance are critical considerations in today's data-driven landscape. Natural language querying can be implemented within a robust data governance framework to ensure that organizations maintain control over their data and comply with relevant regulations and security requirements.

Access controls and permissions can be embedded in the system, allowing administrators to define and govern who has access to specific data sets or repositories. This ensures that only authorized users can interact with sensitive or confidential information, mitigating the risk of unauthorized access or data breaches.

Additionally, natural language querying systems can incorporate data ownership, which assigns responsibility and accountability for specific datasets or data sources. This ownership framework helps organizations maintain data integrity, visibility, and control, ensuring that users are accountable for the data they access and analyze.

Query logs play a crucial role in maintaining data governance and compliance. By analyzing these logs, organizations can gain visibility into how data is being used and accessed. This analysis enables organizations to monitor data usage patterns, identify potential anomalies or security breaches, and address any compliance issues promptly. Moreover, query logs serve as essential audit trails, providing a historical record of data interactions, contributing to compliance with regulatory requirements, such as GDPR or HIPAA.

By implementing natural language querying within a robust data governance framework, organizations can enhance their ability to adhere to data governance and compliance policies. This not only ensures the security and integrity of the data but also helps build trust with customers, partners, and regulatory bodies.

In summary, natural language querying can be implemented in a way that aligns with an organization's data governance and compliance requirements. By incorporating access controls, permissions, data ownership, and query logs, organizations can maintain control over sensitive data, track data usage, and ensure compliance with regulations. This level of data governance not only protects the organization and its stakeholders but also instills confidence in the data analytics process and helps foster a culture of trust when leveraging data for decision-making.

Conclusion

In conclusion, natural language querying is a game-changing technology that empowers organizations to unlock the full potential of their enterprise data repository. By harnessing the power of everyday language, organizations can enable users across various roles and departments to directly access and interact with their data, without relying on technical experts or complex querying languages.

The benefits of natural language querying are substantial. First and foremost, it increases productivity and efficiency by reducing the dependency on technical teams and streamlining workflows. Business users can simply ask questions in plain language and receive instant answers, enabling faster decision-making and driving organizational agility.

Furthermore, natural language querying promotes the democratization of data within the organization. Business users, regardless of their technical background, can tap into the power of data analytics and draw meaningful insights. This fosters a data-driven culture throughout the organization, as users at all levels can independently access and interpret the data.

Time-to-insights is significantly reduced with natural language querying. Real-time answers to questions allow users to make informed decisions in a timely manner. This agility enhances the organization's ability to respond to market changes, identify emerging trends, and seize new opportunities.

Enhanced collaboration and data exploration are also facilitated by natural language querying. Users can understand, access, and share data through conversational interfaces, encouraging knowledge exchange within teams. This collaborative approach can lead to the discovery of hidden patterns, insights, and correlations that might have otherwise been missed.

Finally, natural language querying can be built on a robust data governance framework, ensuring compliance with regulations and data security. Access controls, permissions, data ownership, and query logs can be implemented to maintain control over sensitive data and monitor data integrity.

How to Successfully Implement AI in the Enterprise: A Comprehensive Guide

ARTIFICIAL INTELLIGENCE (AI) HAS EMERGED as a game-changer in the business world, offering tremendous potential for organizations to enhance efficiency, improve decision-making, and drive innovation. However, implementing AI in your enterprise requires careful planning and execution to ensure successful adoption and maximize its benefits. In this chapter, we will provide a comprehensive guide on how to implement AI in your enterprise effectively.

Step 1: Define Clear Business Goals

Before implementing AI in your organization, you must define clear business goals that align with your overall strategy. It is crucial to identify the specific pain points or challenges that your organization seeks to address through AI. This step sets the foundation for successful AI implementation.

Identifying your business goals enables you to focus your AI initiatives on areas where it will have the most significant impact. It allows you to align your AI strategy with your broader business objectives and ensure that AI is seen as an enabler for achieving those goals.

To define clear business goals for AI implementation, follow these steps:

1. Identify Pain Points: Assess your organization and identify areas where you are facing challenges or inefficiencies. This could include operational inefficiencies, customer satisfaction issues, or the need to automate manual processes. Understanding these pain points will guide you in determining how AI can help address them.
2. Prioritize Goals: Once you have identified the pain points, prioritize them based on their potential impact on your organization. Determine

which goals are critical for improving efficiency, enhancing customer experience, or driving growth.

3. Align with Business Strategy: Ensure your AI goals align with your broader business strategy. Consider how AI can support your overall mission and objectives. For example, if your business strategy focuses on providing personalized customer experiences, one of your AI goals could be to develop a recommendation engine to enhance customer satisfaction and drive sales.

4. Set Measurable Objectives: Clearly define the objectives you want to achieve with AI implementation. Ensure that these objectives are measurable and can be tracked over time. This will enable you to monitor progress and evaluate the success of your AI initiatives.

5. Communicate and Gain Buy-in: Once you have defined your business goals for AI implementation, communicate them throughout the organization. Ensure everyone understands the objectives and how AI fits into the overall strategy. Gain alignment from key stakeholders to create a shared vision and support for the implementation process.

By defining clear business goals, you provide a clear direction for your AI initiatives. This clarity helps you prioritize and allocate resources effectively, ensuring that AI implementation is strategic and aligned with your organization's objectives. It also sets the stage for measuring the success and impact of AI on your business.

Step 2: Assess Readiness and Capabilities

Implementing AI in your organization requires a thorough assessment of your readiness and capabilities. This step helps you determine if your organization has the necessary resources, infrastructure, and expertise to adopt AI effectively. It provides valuable insights into whether you have the internal capacity to drive AI implementation or if you need to seek external assistance.

To assess your organization's readiness and capabilities for AI adoption, consider the following factors:

1. Data Availability: Evaluate the availability and quality of your organization's data. AI relies heavily on data to train models and make accurate predictions. Assess if your organization has access to the rel-

evant data required for AI initiatives. Determine whether the data are structured, unstructured, or semi-structured, and identify any data gaps that need to be addressed.

2. Infrastructure: Examine your organization's current IT infrastructure and determine if it can support AI implementation. Consider factors such as computing power, storage capabilities, and network bandwidth. Assess if any upgrades or enhancements are required to handle the increased computational demands of AI algorithms.

3. Workforce Expertise: Evaluate the skills and expertise of your workforce in relation to AI. Determine if you have employees who understand AI concepts, algorithms, and technologies. Assess if you have data scientists, machine learning engineers, or AI specialists in-house. Identify any skill gaps that need to be addressed through training or recruitment.

4. Resource Allocation: Determine if your organization has the financial and human resources to support AI implementation. Implementing AI involves investment in technology, training, and talent. Assess if you have the budget to acquire or develop AI tools and systems. Evaluate if you have the capacity to allocate dedicated personnel to drive AI initiatives.

5. External Partnerships: Consider if partnering with external providers or consultants is necessary to augment your organization's AI capabilities. External expertise can provide valuable insights, guidance, and support throughout the AI implementation process. Evaluate potential partners based on their domain knowledge, experience, and track record.

By conducting a comprehensive assessment of your organization's readiness and capabilities, you gain a clear understanding of the resources and expertise available for successful AI adoption. This assessment helps you identify any gaps that need to be addressed, whether through training existing employees, hiring new talent, or partnering with external experts. It also provides a realistic view of the investment required for AI implementation and ensures that your organization is well-prepared for the challenges and opportunities that come with integrating AI into your business operations.

Step 3: Identify Suitable AI Use Cases

Identifying suitable AI use cases is a critical step in the AI implementation process, as it ensures that the technology aligns with your organization's needs and goals. By brainstorming potential applications of AI across different departments or functions, you can uncover areas where AI can provide the most significant value and address critical pain points.

To identify suitable AI use cases, follow these steps:

1. Brainstorm Potential Applications: Gather key stakeholders from various departments or functions within your organization and conduct brainstorming sessions. Encourage participants to think creatively about how AI can be applied to solve specific challenges or enhance existing processes. Consider areas such as customer service, supply chain management, finance, marketing, or operations.

2. Evaluate Potential Value: Assess the potential value that each use case offers to your organization. Consider factors such as cost savings, efficiency gains, improved customer experience, or increased revenue. Prioritize use cases that have the most significant impact or align closely with your strategic objectives.

3. Address Critical Pain Points: Identify use cases that directly address critical pain points or challenges faced by your organization. These could include areas with bottlenecks, manual intensive processes, or areas where decision-making could benefit from advanced analytics and predictive capabilities. Focus on use cases that have the potential to drive meaningful improvements in performance or outcomes.

4. Consider Feasibility: Evaluate the technical feasibility of each use case. Assess whether the necessary data is available, whether the required technology and infrastructure are in place, and if the use case aligns with your organization's timeline and resources.

5. Involve Key Stakeholders: Engage key stakeholders throughout the process of identifying suitable use cases. This ensures that the selected AI initiatives have support and buy-in from relevant departments or teams. Collaborate with these stakeholders to further refine and validate the use cases before moving forward with implementation.

6. Prioritize Use Cases: Once you have generated a list of potential AI use cases, prioritize them based on their potential value, feasibility, and alignment with your organizational goals. Select a few use cases

that offer a good balance of impact and complexity to start with. This approach allows you to gain early wins and build momentum before expanding to more comprehensive AI implementations.

By identifying suitable AI use cases, you can ensure that your AI implementation efforts are focused on areas with the greatest potential impact and return on investment. This step helps you tailor AI solutions to address specific pain points or challenges within your organization and sets the stage for a successful and targeted implementation.

Step 4: Data Strategy and Governance

Developing a robust data strategy and implementing effective data governance are crucial steps for successful AI implementation. A solid data foundation ensures that the right data are available, accessible, and of high quality for your AI use cases. It also ensures compliance with privacy regulations, data security, and ethical considerations.

To develop an effective data strategy and implement proper data governance, consider the following:

1. Identify Data Sources and Types: Determine the data sources and types required for your AI use cases. This includes both internal data from within your organization and external data from third-party sources. Identify structured and unstructured data sources that can provide valuable insights for AI algorithms.

2. Assess Data Quality and Completeness: Evaluate the quality and completeness of your data. Poor data quality can result in inaccurate AI models and predictions. Assess factors such as accuracy, consistency, relevance, and reliability. Identify any data gaps or issues that need to be addressed and develop a plan to improve data quality.

3. Ensure Data Accessibility: Ensure that the data needed for your AI initiatives are accessible by the relevant teams and systems. Consider data integration and data engineering to aggregate, clean, and transform data into a centralized and accessible format. Implement data warehousing or data lakes to store and organize large volumes of data.

4. Implement Data Governance Framework: Establish a data governance framework to ensure proper management, usage, and protection of

data. Define roles and responsibilities for data ownership and stewardship within your organization. Implement policies and procedures to ensure compliance with privacy regulations, data security, and ethical considerations.

5. Ensure Privacy and Security: Safeguard the privacy and security of your data. Implement measures to protect sensitive and personally identifiable information. Adhere to relevant privacy regulations, such as GDPR or CCPA, and develop protocols for data anonymization or pseudonymization when necessary.
6. Ethical Considerations: Consider the ethical implications of using AI and data. Establish guidelines and principles for responsible AI usage. Address biases in data collection and model development. Ensure transparency and fairness in AI decision-making processes.
7. Continuous Data Improvement: Implement processes for continuously monitoring and improving data quality. Regularly assess and validate data sources and update data collection methods as needed. Invest in data analytics tools and techniques to derive actionable insights from your data.

A strong data strategy and effective data governance are foundational elements for successful AI implementation. By ensuring the availability, accessibility, and quality of data, organizations can harness the full potential of AI technologies. Additionally, by adhering to data privacy and security regulations and considering ethical considerations, organizations can build trust and confidence in their AI initiatives.

Step 5: Build or Acquire AI Solutions

Once you have prioritized your AI use cases and defined your data strategy, the next step is to determine whether to build or acquire AI solutions. This decision depends on various factors such as the complexity of the use case, available resources, cost considerations, scalability requirements, and customization needs.

1. Assess In-house Capabilities: Evaluate your organization's in-house capabilities in terms of technical expertise and resources. Determine if you have the necessary talent and infrastructure to build AI solutions from scratch. Assess the expertise of your data scientists, engineers,

and developers who will be involved in AI development.

2. Consider Open-Source Frameworks: Explore open-source AI frameworks such as TensorFlow, PyTorch, or scikit-learn. These frameworks provide a foundation for building AI models and can be customized to suit your specific use cases. Utilizing open-source technologies can reduce costs and provide flexibility in development.

3. Evaluate Cloud-based AI Platforms: Consider leveraging cloud-based AI platforms such as Amazon Web Services (AWS), Google Cloud AI, or Microsoft Azure. These platforms offer pre-trained AI models and scalable infrastructure, allowing you to accelerate AI development without the need for extensive in-house resources. Assess the pricing structure, ease of use, and integration capabilities of different cloud providers.

4. Partner with AI Technology Providers: Assess the option of partnering with AI technology providers or consulting firms. These providers specialize in AI technologies, tools, and expertise. Partnering with them can expedite AI implementation and ensure access to advanced AI capabilities. Evaluate their domain knowledge, experience, and track record to find the right partner for your specific use cases.

5. Cost and Scalability Considerations: Evaluate the cost implications of building or acquiring AI solutions. Building AI solutions in-house requires investment in talent, infrastructure, and ongoing maintenance. Acquiring solutions, whether through open-source frameworks or partnerships, may involve licensing or subscription costs. Consider the long-term scalability requirements and how well the chosen option can accommodate future growth and evolving AI needs.

6. Customization Options: Consider the level of customization required for your AI use cases. Determine if the flexibility provided by open-source frameworks or cloud-based platforms is sufficient for your needs. Assess whether ready-to-use solutions offered by technology providers can be customized to suit your specific requirements.

Ultimately, the decision to build or acquire AI solutions depends on the unique needs and resources of your organization. In some cases, building AI solutions in-house may provide more control and customization options, especially for complex or industry-specific use cases. However, when resources are limited or speed to market is crucial, acquiring AI solutions through open-source frameworks or partnerships can be a cost-effective and efficient approach.

Carefully evaluate the available options, considering factors such as cost, scalability, customization, and available expertise, to select the most suitable approach for each AI use case identified in your organization's strategy.

Step 6: Pilot Testing and Proof of Concept

Before fully deploying AI solutions across your organization, it is crucial to conduct pilot tests and proofs of concept. This step allows you to validate the feasibility, performance, and impact of your AI initiatives in a controlled environment. It provides an opportunity to gather valuable feedback, measure key performance indicators (KPIs), and refine your approach based on the results obtained during the pilot phase.

Here are the key aspects to consider during pilot testing and proof of concept:

1. Define Objectives: Clearly define the objectives and success criteria for the pilot tests. Determine the specific goals you want to achieve and the KPIs that will be used to measure success. These objectives will guide the evaluation process and help you assess the effectiveness of your AI solution.

2. Select Representative Use Cases: Choose a few representative use cases or scenarios to include in the pilot tests. Select use cases that showcase the potential of AI and align with your business objectives. These use cases should have a significant impact on addressing pain points or improving key processes within your organization.

3. Establish a Controlled Environment: Create a controlled environment for the pilot tests where you can closely monitor and evaluate the performance of your AI solution. This includes gathering the necessary data, setting up the required infrastructure, and ensuring that the selected use cases are simulated or run in a controlled setting.

4. Measure Key Performance Indicators: Define the specific KPIs that will be used to evaluate the success of the pilot tests. These KPIs might include accuracy, efficiency gains, cost reduction, customer satisfaction, or any other relevant metrics based on the use case and your organizational goals. Collect data and measure the performance against these indicators.

5. Gather Feedback and Iterate: During the pilot phase, collect feedback from users, stakeholders, and the teams involved in the testing process. Capture their insights, suggestions, and concerns regarding the AI solution's performance, usability, and overall impact. Use this feedback to iterate and refine your approach, making necessary adjustments or improvements.
6. Evaluate Feasibility and Scalability: Assess the feasibility of scaling the AI solution beyond the pilot phase. Consider the technical scalability, cost implications, and any additional infrastructure or data requirements that may arise as the solution is rolled out across the organization. Evaluate the potential impact on other processes and systems within your organization.
7. Document and Share Results: Document the results, lessons learned, and insights gained during the pilot testing phase. Share these findings across your organization to generate awareness and build support for further AI implementation. Ensure that the results and insights inform the decision-making process for the wider adoption of AI solutions.

By conducting pilot tests and proofs of concept, you can validate the effectiveness and suitability of your AI solutions before deploying them organization-wide. This step allows you to identify any issues, limitations, or necessary improvements in a controlled and manageable setting. It also provides an opportunity to learn valuable lessons that can be used to optimize and refine your AI initiatives for maximum impact and success.

Step 7: Implement and Integrate AI Solutions

After successfully completing pilot tests and obtaining valuable insights, it's time to move forward with the implementation and integration of AI solutions across your organization. This step involves creating a comprehensive implementation plan, ensuring smooth integration with existing systems and processes, and managing the transition effectively.

Here are the key considerations for implementing and integrating AI solutions:

1. Develop a Detailed Implementation Plan: Create a detailed plan that outlines the specific tasks, timelines, milestones, and resource allocation

required for the successful implementation of AI solutions. Break down the implementation into manageable phases and establish clear targets for each phase. This plan will serve as a roadmap for the entire implementation process, ensuring an organized and structured approach.

2. Allocate Resources Appropriately: Assign the necessary resources, including personnel, budget, and infrastructure, to support the implementation. Ensure that the team responsible for implementing AI solutions has the required skills, knowledge, and capacity to carry out the tasks effectively. Regularly assess and adjust resource allocation as needed throughout the implementation process.

3. Integration with Existing Systems and Processes: Evaluate how the AI solutions will integrate with your existing systems, infrastructure, and processes. Identify any necessary modifications or adaptations that may be required to ensure smooth integration. Collaborate with relevant teams or departments to minimize disruptions and facilitate a seamless transition.

4. Address Data Integration and Privacy Concerns: Pay close attention to data integration and privacy considerations during the implementation. Ensure that the AI solutions can access and utilize the necessary data effectively. Implement appropriate data integration techniques, such as data pipelines or APIs, to facilitate seamless data flow between systems. Maintain compliance with privacy regulations and establish protocols to protect sensitive data throughout the AI implementation.

5. Communicate and Train Employees: Communicate the implementation plan and goals to employees throughout the organization. Provide clear information about the benefits and impacts of the AI solutions. Conduct comprehensive training programs to familiarize employees with the new AI technology, workflows, and processes. Encourage open communication and address any concerns or resistance that may arise.

6. Monitor Performance and Make Adjustments: Establish mechanisms to monitor the performance of the AI solutions and track their impact on key performance indicators and business objectives. Continuously evaluate how well the implemented AI solutions are meeting the goals set during the initial stages. Make adjustments and refinements as needed to optimize performance and ensure ongoing success.

7. Evaluate Change Management Strategies: Implement effective change management strategies to support employees throughout

the implementation process. Address any changes in roles, tasks, or responsibilities resulting from the implementation of AI solutions. Promote a positive AI culture and encourage employee involvement and collaboration to drive success.

By following a well-defined implementation plan and ensuring seamless integration with existing systems and processes, you can minimize disruptions and achieve a smooth transition to utilizing AI solutions effectively. Ongoing monitoring, evaluation, and adjustment are crucial to optimize performance and drive continuous improvement. With effective change management and training, you can foster a culture that embraces AI and maximizes its potential for transforming your organization.

Step 8: Continuous Monitoring and Evaluation

Implementing AI is not a one-time project but an ongoing process that requires continuous monitoring and evaluation to ensure its effectiveness and maximize its impact on your organization's goals. This step involves establishing a framework for measuring performance, regularly monitoring key performance indicators (KPIs), and continuously reviewing and refining your AI models and algorithms.

Here are the key aspects to consider for continuous monitoring and evaluation of AI initiatives:

1. Define Performance Metrics and KPIs: Identify the specific performance metrics and KPIs that align with your organization's objectives and the goals set during the initial stages of AI implementation. These metrics can include productivity, cost savings, customer satisfaction, revenue growth, or any other relevant measures. Clear definitions and targets for these metrics will provide a benchmark for evaluating the success and impact of your AI initiatives.

2. Establish Monitoring Mechanisms: Implement mechanisms to continuously collect and analyze relevant data to track the performance of your AI solutions against the defined metrics. This may involve setting up automated processes to generate reports, using analytics tools to track real-time data, or leveraging AI-powered monitoring systems. Regularly review and interpret the data to gain insights into the progress and impact of your AI initiatives.

3. Conduct Regular Performance Reviews: Schedule periodic reviews to assess the performance of your AI initiatives. These reviews can be conducted monthly, quarterly, or annually, depending on the nature of your organization and the specific AI use cases. Evaluate the progress made, identify any issues or bottlenecks, and assess if the AI solutions are delivering the expected benefits.

4. Refine AI Models and Algorithms: Continuously review and refine your AI models and algorithms to improve their performance and ensure optimal results. Incorporate new data, insights, or feedback into the AI models and algorithms to enhance their accuracy, efficiency, and predictive capabilities. Consider leveraging techniques such as machine learning retraining or fine-tuning to adapt AI models over time.

5. Seek Feedback from Users and Stakeholders: Actively gather feedback from users, stakeholders, and customers who interact with the AI solutions. Solicit their opinions, suggestions, and experiences to gain a holistic understanding of the impact of AI on their workflows, experiences, and outcomes. Incorporate this feedback into the evaluation process and use it to identify areas for improvement or refinement.

6. Iterate and Update Implementation: Based on the findings from monitoring and evaluation, make iterative improvements and updates to your AI implementation. This may involve modifying processes, adjusting workflows, or enhancing the technology infrastructure supporting AI initiatives. Continuously iterate and update your AI implementation to ensure alignment with evolving business needs and technological advancements.

7. Foster a Culture of Learning and Innovation: Promote a culture of learning, experimentation, and innovation within your organization. Encourage employees to explore new AI techniques, stay updated with advancements in the field, and contribute their ideas for improvement. Create forums for sharing knowledge, best practices, and lessons learned from AI implementation to foster continuous improvement and drive innovation.

By continuously monitoring and evaluating your AI initiatives, you can gain insights into their performance, identify areas for improvement, and maximize your return on investment. This iterative approach allows you to continuously enhance your AI models, align them with changing business needs, and leverage the full potential of AI to drive transformation and success in your organization.

Step 9: Change Management and Employee Training

Implementing AI successfully within an organization requires effective change management and thorough employee training. It is crucial to communicate the benefits of AI to your workforce, address any concerns or resistance, and provide comprehensive training programs to upskill and reskill employees to work alongside AI systems. This step also involves fostering a culture of continuous learning and embracing the possibilities that AI brings to the roles and responsibilities of your employees.

Consider the following aspects when managing change and training employees for AI implementation:

1. Communicate the Benefits of AI: Clearly communicate the benefits of AI to your workforce to create buy-in and alleviate any fears or misconceptions. Explain how AI can enhance productivity, streamline processes, and increase job satisfaction. Emphasize that AI is not meant to replace employees, but rather to augment their capabilities and free up time for more strategic tasks.

2. Address Concerns and Resistance: Recognize that employees may have concerns and resistance to AI implementation. Create a safe and open environment for employees to voice their concerns and address them transparently. Address misconceptions, clarify any potential job displacement concerns, and emphasize that AI is a tool to support employees and enhance their work.

3. Provide Comprehensive Training Programs: Offer comprehensive training programs to equip employees with the necessary AI skills and knowledge. This includes training on AI concepts, algorithms, and technologies, as well as how to effectively work alongside AI systems. Tailor the training to different employee roles and responsibilities, ensuring they understand how AI impacts their specific job functions.

4. Upskill and Reskill Employees: Identify skill gaps within your workforce and design upskilling and reskilling programs to bridge those gaps. Provide employees with opportunities to learn new skills, such as data analysis, AI programming, or AI model interpretation. Foster a culture of continuous learning by providing access to educational resources, workshops, and mentorship.

5. Foster Collaboration and Cross-functional Learning: Encourage collaboration and cross-functional learning among employees to facilitate knowledge-sharing and innovation. Allow employees from different

departments to collaborate on AI projects, promoting a multidisciplinary approach. This helps create a collective understanding of AI's potential and encourages employees to explore new possibilities and ideas.

6. Emphasize Continuous Learning and Adaptability: Embrace a mindset of continuous learning and adaptability within the organization. Encourage employees to stay updated with AI advancements, attend industry events or webinars, and participate in relevant training programs. Create forums for sharing knowledge and experiences related to AI implementation, fostering a culture of innovation and growth.
7. Provide Support and Guidance: Offer ongoing support and guidance to employees as they navigate the changes brought about by AI implementation. Provide mentoring or coaching programs to help employees adapt to new ways of working. Establish channels for feedback and address any challenges or issues that arise promptly.

By effectively managing change and providing comprehensive training, you can ensure employees are prepared for the changes AI implementation brings. This fosters a positive and inclusive culture where employees embrace the possibilities of AI and actively contribute to its successful integration. Engaged and well-trained employees can leverage AI technologies to enhance their work while driving innovation and efficiency within the organization.

Step 10: Stay Updated with AI Advancements

In the ever-evolving landscape of AI, it is crucial to stay updated with the latest advancements, trends, and innovations. By continuously learning about new developments, organizations can seize new opportunities, stay competitive, and make informed decisions regarding their AI strategies. This step involves actively seeking knowledge from various sources, participating in industry events, attending conferences, and leveraging networking opportunities.

Consider the following strategies to stay updated with AI advancements:

1. Follow Trusted Sources: Follow thought leaders, industry experts, and reputable organizations in the field of AI. Subscribe to their blogs, newsletters, and social media accounts to receive regular updates and insights. Stay informed about recent research papers, case studies, and breakthroughs in AI.

2. Engage in Industry Events: Attend conferences, seminars, and workshops specifically focused on AI. These events provide a platform to learn from industry leaders, academics, and practitioners. Attend keynote talks, panel discussions, and breakout sessions to gain insights into cutting-edge AI applications, best practices, and future trends.

3. Participate in Webinars and Online Courses: Take advantage of webinars and online courses that cover various AI topics. These platforms offer flexibility and convenience, allowing you to fit learning into your schedule. Engage with experts, ask questions, and interact with fellow participants to deepen your understanding of AI advancements.

4. Join AI Communities and Forums: Join online communities, forums, and discussion groups that are dedicated to AI. These platforms provide opportunities to connect with like-minded individuals, share knowledge, and engage in conversations around AI advancements. Participate actively, ask questions, and contribute to discussions to enhance your own learning.

5. Collaborate with Research Institutions: Establish collaborations or partnerships with academic and research institutions working in the field of AI. These institutions often conduct research and develop groundbreaking AI technologies. Collaborative initiatives can provide access to the latest research findings, cutting-edge techniques, and potential joint projects that contribute to the advancement of AI.

6. Foster Internal AI Learning Initiatives: Encourage internal learning initiatives within your organization to promote ongoing education and awareness about AI advancements. Establish AI-focused training programs, lunch-and-learn sessions, or knowledge-sharing sessions where employees can discuss and exchange insights about AI. Encourage employees to share posts, papers, or reports they come across to foster continuous learning.

7. Maintain an Agile AI Strategy: As AI evolves rapidly, it is essential to maintain an agile AI strategy that can adapt to emerging trends and advancements. Continuously evaluate and refine your AI roadmap based on new insights and developments. Regularly assess the impact of AI advancements on your industry and business, ensuring that your strategy remains aligned with the changing landscape.

By staying updated with AI advancements, you can ensure that your organization remains at the forefront of AI innovation. This knowledge empowers you to leverage new opportunities, make informed decisions, and effectively implement AI technologies to drive business success. Embracing a continuous learning approach enables you to adapt, evolve, and stay ahead in the ever-changing world of AI.

Conclusion

Implementing AI in your organization is a complex endeavor that requires careful planning, diligent execution, and continuous improvement. By following the comprehensive guide outlined above, you can navigate the AI implementation process with confidence. From defining clear business goals and assessing readiness to identifying suitable use cases, building or acquiring AI solutions, and fostering a culture of continuous learning, each step plays a crucial role in ensuring the successful integration of AI into your organization.

The potential benefits of AI are vast and extend across industries. By leveraging AI technologies, organizations can enhance operational efficiency, improve decision-making, personalize customer experiences, and drive innovation. However, it is important to approach AI implementation with a clear understanding of your unique business goals and challenges. This ensures that AI initiatives align with your overall strategy and deliver value.

As AI continues to evolve rapidly, staying updated with advancements and trends is paramount. By actively seeking knowledge, attending industry events, and engaging with experts, you can stay ahead of the curve and seize new opportunities that arise from cutting-edge AI applications. Maintaining an agile AI strategy allows you to adapt and respond to emerging trends, ensuring that your organization remains at the forefront of AI-driven innovation.

Measuring ROI and Impact of AI Initiatives

Introduction

IN TODAY'S BUSINESS LANDSCAPE, where technology is constantly evolving, Return on Investment (ROI) has become a crucial factor in determining the success of any investment. With the rise of artificial intelligence (AI), businesses are increasingly investing in AI initiatives to gain a competitive edge. However, measuring the ROI of these initiatives can be complex due to their transformative nature. In this chapter, we will explore the challenges of measuring ROI for AI initiatives and discuss effective ways to assess their impact on business performance.

Understanding AI Initiatives

AI initiatives are at the forefront of technological advancements, offering businesses the opportunity to transform and optimize their operations. These initiatives encompass a wide range of technologies and applications that aim to mimic human intelligence and automate various tasks. Some of the common forms of AI initiatives include machine learning, deep learning, natural language processing, computer vision, and robotics.

Machine learning is a subset of AI that enables computer systems to learn and improve from experience without being explicitly programmed. By using algorithms and statistical models, machine learning systems can analyze large datasets to identify patterns, make predictions, and generate insights. This technology can be used for various applications, such as fraud detection, predictive maintenance, and recommendation systems.

Deep learning, a subset of machine learning, is inspired by the structure and functioning of the human brain. Deep learning models, also known as neural networks, consist of multiple layers of artificial neurons that process data inputs and generate outputs. This technology has proven to be highly effective in tasks such as image recognition, natural language processing, and voice recognition.

Natural language processing (NLP) focuses on enabling computers to understand and interact with human language. This technology enables applications like chatbots, virtual assistants, and language translation systems. NLP can help automate customer support, enhance search functionality, and carry out personalized interactions with users.

Computer vision involves training computers to interpret and understand visual information from images and videos. This technology has numerous applications, such as facial recognition, object detection, and autonomous driving. It can be used to automate surveillance, improve quality control in manufacturing, and enhance medical diagnostics.

By leveraging AI initiatives, businesses can gain various benefits that directly impact their performance and bottom line. Improved decision-making is one of the key advantages. AI-powered systems can process and analyze vast amounts of data quickly, uncovering patterns and insights that humans may miss. This enables businesses to make more informed decisions based on data-driven insights, leading to better outcomes and competitive advantages.

Automation is another critical aspect of AI initiatives. By automating repetitive and mundane tasks, businesses can free up human resources to focus on more strategic and creative endeavors. This not only improves operational efficiency but also reduces costs and improves productivity.

AI also facilitates the creation of personalized customer experiences. Through AI-powered recommendation systems and personalized messaging, businesses can tailor their offerings to individual customers' preferences and needs. This personalization can result in not only higher conversion rates but also increased customer satisfaction and improved customer loyalty.

Furthermore, AI initiatives can optimize business processes by identifying bottlenecks, predicting maintenance needs, and optimizing resource allocation. This can lead to significant cost savings, time efficiencies, and overall operational improvements.

AI initiatives encompass a wide range of technologies and applications that aim to mimic human intelligence and automate tasks. By leveraging AI, businesses can make better decisions, automate repetitive tasks, create personalized customer experiences, and improve overall operational efficiency. With these benefits, AI is rapidly becoming a crucial aspect of business strategies across various industries.

The Complexity of Measuring ROI for AI Initiatives

Measuring the ROI for AI initiatives is a complex task that requires careful consideration of various factors. Unlike traditional investments, AI initiatives often involve substantial upfront costs for infrastructure, data acquisition, and talent acquisition. These costs can include investments in high-performance computing systems, data storage and processing capabilities, and hiring skilled data scientists or AI specialists.

Furthermore, the returns from AI investments are not always immediate or direct, which makes it challenging to quantify their impact on ROI. AI initiatives often involve a learning phase where algorithms are trained on historical data to improve their performance. This initial phase may not yield immediate financial benefits but is necessary to optimize the AI system and achieve long-term gains. As a result, measuring the ROI of AI initiatives requires a longer-term perspective and an understanding of the potential future benefits.

Ongoing maintenance and training costs also pose a challenge when measuring ROI for AI initiatives. AI systems require continuous updates, data cleaning, and model retraining to stay effective and adapt to evolving business needs. These maintenance and training costs can be significant and must be factored into the calculation of ROI. However, estimating the future costs accurately can be difficult, as they depend on various factors such as the complexity of the AI system, data quality, and the rate of technological advancements.

Additionally, quantifying the intangible benefits generated by AI initiatives adds another layer of complexity to measuring ROI. While tangible benefits such as cost savings or revenue increase can be measured directly, intangible benefits such as improved brand reputation, enhanced customer loyalty, or increased market share are more challenging to quantify in monetary terms. These intangible benefits, although important for overall business performance, often require qualitative assessment methods such as surveys, focus groups, or sentiment analysis to gather insights.

To illustrate the complexities of measuring AI ROI, let's consider the example of Company XYZ. They invested heavily in implementing an AI-powered chatbot to handle customer inquiries. The chatbot successfully reduced the response times and improved operational efficiency. However, quantifying the impact of these improvements on ROI proved challenging due to the lack of a robust measurement framework. Each business has unique metrics and KPIs that align with their objectives, making it essential to establish a clear framework to measure the impact of AI investments accurately. We discuss below a new, effective framework they could use.

Overcoming the complexity of measuring AI ROI requires a comprehensive approach. It involves carefully considering the upfront costs, ongoing maintenance and training costs, the long-term perspective, and the intangible benefits that AI initiatives can generate. By defining clear metrics and measurement frameworks specific to the business context, organizations can gain a deeper understanding of the true impact and ROI of their AI investments. This understanding is crucial for making informed decisions, optimizing resource allocation, and driving successful AI implementations.

Frameworks for Measuring ROI of AI

To effectively measure the ROI of AI initiatives, a comprehensive framework that accounts for various factors is necessary. While existing models and frameworks have been developed, they often have limitations in capturing the full impact of AI initiatives. Therefore, we propose a new framework that takes a holistic approach to measure the ROI of AI initiatives.

1. Identify Costs: The first step in the framework is to identify and quantify all relevant costs associated with the AI initiative. This includes infrastructure costs such as hardware, software, and cloud services. It also includes data-related costs such as data acquisition, preprocessing, and storage. Additionally, talent acquisition and training costs for data scientists and AI specialists should be considered.

2. Assess Benefits: Next, quantify the benefits generated by the AI initiative. Tangible benefits can include cost savings through automation, reduced errors, or increased revenue from improved decision-making. These benefits should be quantified in monetary terms whenever possible.

3. Consider Efficiency Gains: AI initiatives can often result in significant improvements in operational efficiency. For example, automating repetitive tasks can free up employee time, allowing them to focus on higher-value activities. Quantify the time and cost savings achieved through efficiency gains.

4. Measure Customer Satisfaction Improvements: AI applications like chatbots or recommendation engines can enhance the customer experience and satisfaction. Collect and analyze customer feedback, ratings, and reviews to quantify the impact on customer satisfaction metrics.

5. Capture Intangible Benefits: Intangible benefits, such as improved brand reputation, enhanced customer loyalty, or increased market share, are essential to consider. These benefits may be more challenging to quantify in monetary terms but can still be assessed through qualitative methods like surveys or sentiment analysis.

6. Calculate ROI: To calculate the ROI, subtract the total costs from the total benefits and divide by the total costs. This will give you a percentage that represents the return generated by the AI initiative relative to the investment made.

It is important to note that the proposed framework should be tailored to suit the specific context and goals of each AI initiative. The metrics and measurements used may vary depending on the industry, organization, and objectives. Regular monitoring and evaluation of the initiative's performance should also be conducted to ensure ongoing optimization and potential adjustments to the ROI calculation.

By using this comprehensive framework, businesses can gain a more accurate understanding of the actual returns generated by their AI investments. This will enable informed decision-making, resource allocation optimization, and a clearer assessment of the impact of AI initiatives on business performance.

Assessing the Impact of AI on Business Performance

Assessing the impact of AI on business performance is crucial in understanding the value and effectiveness of your AI initiatives. To evaluate this impact, you need to define relevant performance metrics that align with their goals, industry, and specific AI applications. Here are key areas where AI can have a significant impact on business performance:

1. Efficiency: AI has the potential to automate repetitive tasks and streamline processes, leading to increased efficiency. By leveraging AI-powered technologies, businesses can not only optimize resource allocation but also reduce manual errors, and enhance operational workflows. Key metrics that can be used to assess efficiency improvements include time saved, reduction in costs, and increased throughput.

2. Effectiveness: AI can significantly enhance decision-making capabilities by analyzing large volumes of data, identifying patterns, and generating actionable insights. By providing accurate predictions and recommendations, AI enables businesses to make more informed and strategic decisions. Metrics to measure effectiveness can include improvements in forecasting accuracy, better alignment of resources, and increased profitability.

3. Customer Satisfaction: AI-powered solutions can personalize customer experiences, leading to higher customer satisfaction and improved loyalty. In addition, AI enables businesses to better understand customer needs, delivering targeted recommendations and providing efficient customer support. Metrics to measure customer satisfaction may include Net Promoter Score (NPS), customer retention rates, and customer feedback ratings.

To assess the impact of AI initiatives on business performance, a combination of quantitative and qualitative methods can be employed. Quantitative methods involve analyzing specific metrics and KPIs. For example, businesses can track cost reduction percentages, revenue uplift, customer retention rates, or improvements in operational efficiency. These quantitative measures provide tangible evidence of the impact of AI on business performance.

Qualitative methods are equally important to capture the intangible benefits of AI initiatives. Gathering customer feedback through surveys, interviews, or online sentiment analysis can provide insights into customer satisfaction, brand perception, and customer loyalty. This qualitative data helps in understanding the emotional and experiential impact of AI on customer interactions, which can be difficult to measure with quantitative metrics alone.

Real-life use cases of successful AI implementation can provide inspiration and guidance for businesses aiming to assess the impact of AI on their performance. For example, Amazon's recommendation engine, which utilizes AI algorithms to personalize product recommendations, has significantly improved the overall customer experience and increased sales. And Netflix's AI-powered content discovery system has transformed the way users find and engage with content, enhancing customer satisfaction and retention. In addition, Google's AI-driven search algorithms continuously evolve to provide accurate and relevant search results, improving user experiences and increasing user engagement.

By utilizing a combination of quantitative and qualitative methods and analyzing real-life case studies, businesses can gain a comprehensive understanding of the impact of AI on their performance. This information is essential for making data-driven decisions, optimizing AI initiatives, and further enhancing business outcomes.

Factors to Consider when Investing in AI

When investing in AI initiatives, several factors should be considered to ensure alignment with your organization's business strategy and mitigate potential risks. These factors include:

1. Alignment with Business Strategy: Prior to investing in AI initiatives, it is essential to align them with your organization's overall business strategy and objectives. By identifying specific areas where AI can create value, you can prioritize investments that align with your long-term goals. This alignment ensures that AI initiatives complement existing processes and systems, driving synergy and optimizing organizational efficiency.

2. Risk Assessment and Management: Investing in AI carries certain risks and uncertainties. It is crucial to conduct a thorough risk assessment to identify potential challenges and mitigate associated risks. This assessment should consider technical risks related to algorithmic accuracy, data quality, and infrastructure reliability. Additionally, ethical and legal risks associated with privacy, bias, and accountability must be addressed. Establishing a robust risk management strategy will help in proactively managing and mitigating potential issues.

3. Ethical Considerations: Businesses must prioritize ethical considerations when investing in AI. This involves ensuring that AI initiatives are implemented in a responsible and transparent manner. Organizations should prioritize user privacy, comply with relevant regulations, and ensure fairness and accountability in AI algorithms and decision-making processes. Transparent communication regarding the use of AI, data collection, and privacy practices is crucial for building trust with your customers and stakeholders.

4. Talent and Skills: Investing in AI requires access to skilled professionals with expertise in areas such as data science, machine learning, and AI development. Organizations should assess their current talent pool and identify potential skill gaps. Based on this assessment, businesses can determine whether to hire new talent, upskill existing employees, or collaborate with external partners and AI service providers to ensure the successful implementation and management of AI initiatives.

5. Scalability and Flexibility: When investing in AI, it is important to consider the scalability and flexibility of your chosen solutions. AI technology and algorithms should have the capability to scale in line with your organization's needs and accommodate future growth. Additionally, the chosen AI solutions should be adaptable to evolving business requirements and changes in the competitive landscape, ensuring that your investments remain relevant and valuable over time.

6. Continuous Learning and Adaptation: AI is a rapidly evolving field, and investing in AI initiatives requires a commitment to continuous learning and adaptation. Businesses should foster a culture of experimentation and learning, encouraging teams to explore new AI technologies and approaches. This enables you to stay abreast of the latest advancements and adapt your strategies as AI technology progresses.

By considering these factors, you can make informed investment decisions and maximize the potential benefits of AI initiatives while mitigating associated risks. Strategic alignment, risk management, ethical considerations, talent acquisition, scalability, and continuous learning are crucial to successfully investing in AI and harnessing its transformative potential.

Conclusion

Investing in artificial intelligence (AI) initiatives has become increasingly important for businesses to gain a competitive edge. However, measuring the return on investment (ROI) of these initiatives presents unique challenges. The complex nature of AI, coupled with upfront costs, intangible benefits, and ongoing maintenance, requires businesses to adopt effective methods for assessing the impact of AI on business performance and measuring its ROI.

Understanding AI initiatives is the first step towards evaluating their impact on business performance. AI encompasses various technologies like machine learning, deep learning, and natural language processing, which can benefit businesses by improving decision-making, automating tasks, personalizing customer experiences, and enhancing operational efficiency.

However, measuring the ROI of AI initiatives is not a straightforward task. Businesses face challenges in quantifying the returns due to factors like upfront costs, delayed benefits, ongoing maintenance, and intangible benefits. To overcome these challenges, we have proposed a new comprehensive framework in this chapter. This framework considers factors like infrastructure costs, data quality and availability, talent acquisition and training costs, operational efficiency gains, customer satisfaction improvements, and intangible benefits. By adopting this holistic approach, businesses can accurately assess the impact of their AI investments.

Assessing the impact of AI on business performance is a crucial step in measuring its ROI. This involves defining relevant performance metrics in areas such as efficiency, effectiveness, and customer satisfaction. Quantitative methods like cost reduction percentages, revenue uplift, and operational efficiency improvements, along with qualitative methods like customer surveys and sentiment analysis, can be employed to evaluate the impact.

Real-life examples of successful AI implementations, such as Amazon's recommendation engine, Netflix's content discovery, and Google's search algorithms, demonstrate the positive impact of AI on various aspects of business performance.

When investing in AI initiatives, businesses must consider factors like strategic alignment, risk assessment, ethical considerations, talent acquisition, scalability, and continuous learning. Aligning AI investments with the organization's business strategy, managing risks, ensuring ethical implementation, acquiring the right talent, and focusing on scalability and flexibility are key to maximizing the benefits of AI initiatives.

In conclusion, measuring the ROI of AI initiatives and assessing their impact on business performance are vital for informed decision making. Our proposed framework provides a comprehensive approach to measure ROI by considering both tangible and intangible benefits. By evaluating the impact of AI on business performance and considering various factors in AI investments, businesses can make informed decisions, optimize resource allocation, and harness the transformative potential of AI. Embracing the challenge of effectively measuring AI ROI is essential as AI continues to revolutionize various industries, enabling businesses to stay competitive in the rapidly evolving technological landscape.

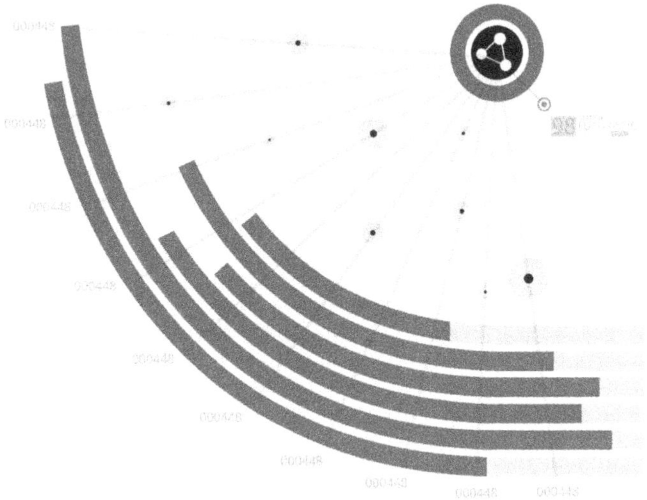

CASE STUDIES

Please visit **C1M.ai/AI-case-studies** today for detailed case studies showcasing how we've helped businesses like yours succeed.

Transforming Your Call Center with Artificial Intelligence: A Project Plan

Introduction

As technology continues to advance, incorporating artificial intelligence (AI) into call center operations has become an attractive option for businesses seeking improved efficiency and customer experience. However, it is essential to strike a balance between automated interactions and maintaining the human touch that customers value. In this chapter, we will outline a step-by-step project plan for transforming your call center into a hybrid model that combines AI technologies with human interactions.

Step 1: Define objectives and key performance indicators (KPIs)

To ensure a successful call center transformation project, it is essential to start by clearly defining your objectives and establishing key performance indicators (KPIs) that align with those objectives. This step will help set the course for the rest of the project and provide a framework for measuring progress and success.

1.1 Identify Objectives

Begin by identifying the specific objectives you aim to achieve through the call center transformation. These objectives should be aligned with your overall business goals and should address pain points or areas in need of improvement within your current call center operations. Common objectives in a call center transformation project may include:

1. Reducing Average Handle Time (AHT): AHT measures the average time it takes for an agent to handle a customer interaction. By reducing AHT, you can improve operational efficiency, handle more calls, and increase customer satisfaction.

2. Increasing First-Call Resolution (FCR): FCR refers to the percentage of customer inquiries or issues resolved on the first call. Improving FCR reduces customer frustration, eliminates repeat calls, and enhances customer loyalty.

3. Improving Customer Satisfaction (CSAT): CSAT measures the level of customer satisfaction with their call center experience. Enhancing CSAT ensures that customers have a positive interaction and are likely to recommend your company to others.

4. Minimizing Operational Costs: Cost reduction is a common objective in call center transformations. By leveraging AI technologies, you can automate certain tasks, reduce agent workload, and optimize resource allocation, leading to cost savings.

1.2 Establish Measurable KPIs

Once you have defined your objectives, it is critical to establish KPIs that can effectively track progress toward those objectives. These KPIs should be specific, measurable, achievable, relevant, and time-bound (SMART). Here are some examples of KPIs that align with the objectives mentioned above:

1. AHT KPIs: Average Handle Time (AHT) per agent, AHT by call type, or AHT trend over time.

2. FCR KPIs: First-Call Resolution rate, FCR by agent or call type, or customer feedback related to FCR.

3. CSAT KPIs: Customer satisfaction survey scores, CSAT by agent or team, or CSAT improvement rate.

4. Cost KPIs: Cost per call, cost-per-contact, or cost savings achieved through automation.

Remember that KPIs should be chosen based on your specific objectives and can be adjusted as needed throughout the project. Regularly reviewing and analyzing these KPIs will provide valuable insights into the transformation's progress and enable you to make informed decisions and adjustments along the way.

1.3 Communicate and Align Objectives and KPIs

Once you have defined and established your objectives and KPIs, it is crucial to communicate them effectively to all stakeholders involved in the call center transformation. This includes senior management, call center managers, agents, and any external vendors or partners. Ensuring that everyone understands and aligns with the objectives and KPIs will foster a shared vision and a unified approach towards achieving the desired outcomes.

Additionally, consider incorporating the objectives and KPIs into performance management systems to incentivize and motivate agents to meet the set targets. Regularly share progress updates and celebrate successes to maintain momentum and engagement throughout the transformation process.

By clearly defining objectives and establishing measurable KPIs, you set a solid foundation for your call center transformation project. These objectives and KPIs will guide your decisions, help track progress, and ultimately enable you to achieve a more efficient call center that effectively combines AI technologies with the human touch your customers value.

Step 2: Conduct a thorough assessment of your current call center

Before diving into the implementation of AI technologies, it is vital to conduct a comprehensive assessment of your current call center operations. This assessment will help you gain a clear understanding of the strengths, weaknesses, and pain points within your existing system. By analyzing call volumes, customer inquiries, resources, technology capabilities, and bottlenecks, you can identify opportunities for improvement and determine how AI can complement or enhance existing processes.

2.1 Analyze Call Volumes and Patterns

Start by examining call volumes over a specific period, such as a month or quarter, to identify any trends or patterns. This analysis will provide insights into peak hours, seasonality, and overall call volume distribution. Understanding call patterns will help you optimize staffing levels, resource allocation, and scheduling, ensuring sufficient coverage during high-demand periods.

2.2 Assess Customer Inquiries and Issue Resolution

Review the types of customer inquiries received at your call center. Categorize and analyze them to identify common issues, frequent questions, and areas that require additional attention. This assessment will aid in determining suitable AI technologies, such as chatbots or virtual agents, for handling routine or repetitive inquiries, allowing human agents to focus on more complex or sensitive customer interactions where empathy and critical thinking are crucial.

2.3 Evaluate Existing Resources and Technology Capabilities

Assess your current resources, including team size, skill sets, and agent performance. Consider whether these resources align with the desired transformation objectives and whether additional hiring or training is required. Evaluate the technology infrastructure, including your current call center software, CRM systems, and data management capabilities. Assess whether your existing technologies can integrate with AI tools seamlessly or whether upgrades or replacements are necessary.

2.4 Identify Pain Points and Bottlenecks

Identify pain points or bottlenecks within your current call center operations. These may include long wait times, high abandonment rates, excessive transfers, or low agent productivity. Examine call flow, agent workflows, and system limitations that may be contributing to these issues. Understand the underlying causes to determine how AI technologies can alleviate these pain points, streamline processes, and improve overall efficiency.

2.5 Determine AI Opportunities

Based on the assessment of your call center's current state, there are various areas where AI can be effectively integrated to complement and enhance existing processes. Here are examples of how AI technologies can be leveraged in a call center setting:

1. Chatbots for Self-Service: Implement AI-powered chatbots that can handle repetitive inquiries and provide self-service options to customers. These chatbots can assist with frequently asked questions, provide account information, process basic transactions, and help customers navigate through your website or mobile app.

2. Sentiment Analysis: Utilize AI technologies for sentiment analysis to assess and understand the emotional states of customers during interactions. Sentiment analysis looks at speech patterns, word choice, and tone to help identify customer moods and provide real-time feedback to agents. This enables agents to tailor their responses and interactions more effectively to meet customer needs and expectations.

3. Voice Recognition for Call Routing: Integrate speech recognition technology to automatically route calls to the most appropriate agent or department based on the caller's needs. Voice recognition capabilities can identify keywords or phrases from the customer's voice input, enabling efficient call routing and minimizing the need for customers to explain their issues multiple times.

4. Predictive Analytics for Demand Forecasting: Leverage predictive analytics to forecast call volumes and customer demand based on historical data. By accurately predicting call volumes, you can optimize staffing levels, ensure adequate agent availability, and improve resource allocation. This helps to prevent understaffed or overstaffed situations, leading to cost savings and enhanced customer satisfaction.

5. Co-browsing and Screen Sharing: Introduce AI-powered tools that enable agents to co-browse or share screens with customers in real-time. This feature allows agents to guide customers through complex processes, troubleshoot technical issues, or provide step-by-step assistance. It enhances the customer experience by offering personalized support as if the agent is virtually present with the customer.

6. Virtual Assistants for Agent Support: Implement virtual assistants or AI-powered tools that provide real-time assistance to agents during customer interactions. These tools can analyze customer data, suggest responses or scripts based on past interactions, provide relevant product information, or offer upsell or cross-sell recommendations. Virtual assistants enhance agent performance and empower them to deliver more personalized and efficient service.

7. Speech Analytics for Quality Assurance: Deploy speech analytics to analyze and evaluate agent-customer conversations. AI technologies can automatically transcribe and analyze calls, detecting keywords, phrases, and patterns indicative of positive or negative customer experiences. This data can be used for quality assurance purposes, agent training, and identifying areas for improvement.

Remember, the specific AI opportunities for your call center will depend on your unique needs, challenges, and customer demands. Continuously evaluate emerging AI technologies and assess their applicability to further enhance your call center operations and drive customer satisfaction. Embracing the potential of AI in these various forms can greatly enhance the efficiency, productivity, and overall performance of your call center.

2.6 Document Findings and Recommendations

Document the findings of your assessment and develop a summary report that outlines the pain points, opportunities, and recommended AI technologies for your call center transformation. This report will serve as a valuable reference and guide as you proceed with implementing AI solutions.

By conducting a thorough assessment of your current call center, you can identify areas that need improvement and gain insights into how AI technologies can be strategically integrated. This understanding will help you make informed decisions, develop an effective implementation plan, and ensure a successful transition to a more efficient and customer-centric AI-powered call center.

Step 3: Develop a roadmap for AI integration

Once you have completed the assessment of your current call center and identified the areas where AI technologies can be effectively integrated, it is time to develop a roadmap for the implementation of these technologies. This roadmap will guide the phased integration of AI into your call center operations, ensuring a smooth transition and maximum impact on efficiency and customer experience.

3.1 Identify Low-Risk and High-Value Use Cases

Begin by identifying low-risk and high-value use cases for the initial implementation of AI technologies. These use cases should be areas where AI can provide measurable improvements in efficiency or customer experience without significant disruption or risk. For example, implementing a chatbot for handling frequently asked questions or introducing voice recognition software for call routing can have an immediate positive impact.

3.2 Prioritize Use Cases

Once you have identified the initial use cases, prioritize them based on their potential value and ease of implementation. Consider factors such as the complexity of the problem being addressed, the availability of suitable AI technologies, and the impact on customer satisfaction and operational efficiency. This prioritization will help you focus your efforts and resources on the most impactful use cases first.

3.3 Define Phases and Milestones

Break down the implementation process into phases and establish milestones for each phase. Each phase should include specific objectives, key activities, and timelines. This phased approach will enable you to manage the implementation process more effectively, measure progress, and address any challenges or limitations as they arise.

3.4 Allocate Resources

Determine the resources required for each phase of the AI integration process. This includes assigning dedicated project managers, securing budget for technology acquisition and implementation, and allocating personnel for training and support. Ensure that you have the necessary resources in place to ensure a successful implementation.

3.5 Evaluate Technology Providers

Research and evaluate technology providers that offer AI solutions aligned with the identified use cases. Consider factors such as the provider's reputation, technology capabilities, integration capabilities with your existing systems, cost, and scalability. Engage in discussions and product demos to assess the fit and select the most suitable provider for each phase.

3.6 Pilot and Test

Before rolling out AI technologies across your entire call center, it is advisable to conduct pilot tests to validate their effectiveness and gather insights for further improvement. Select a representative sample of agents and customers to participate in the pilot program. Collect feedback, measure key performance indicators, and refine the AI implementation based on the learnings from the pilot phase.

3.7 Expand Integration

Once the initial pilot phase is successful, gradually expand the integration of AI technologies into other use cases, departments, or teams. Continuously monitor key performance indicators and customer feedback to ensure that the AI systems are delivering the desired results. Make adjustments as necessary and iterate on the implementation process to achieve optimal efficiency and customer satisfaction.

Developing a roadmap for AI integration is a crucial step in transforming your call center into a more efficient and customer-focused environment. By identifying low-risk and high-value use cases, prioritizing implementation, defining phases and milestones, allocating resources, evaluating technology providers, piloting and testing, and gradually expanding integration, you can ensure a smooth transition to an AI-powered call center. This phased approach will help you leverage AI technologies effectively and reap the benefits of improved efficiency, enhanced customer experience, and sustainable growth.

Step 4: Choose the right AI technologies

Selecting the right AI technologies is a crucial step in the transformation of your call center. The success of your project relies on accurately identifying, evaluating, and implementing the AI tools that best align with your objectives and enhance your call center operations. Here are key considerations for choosing the right AI technologies:

4.1 Clearly Define Objectives and Requirements

Referencing the objectives and requirements established in Step 1, clearly define the specific role AI technologies will play in achieving your call center transformation goals. Identify the business problems or pain points you aim to address and determine the capabilities you require from AI solutions.

4.2 Explore Available AI Technologies

Research and explore the wide range of AI technologies available for call center integration. Some common AI tools include:

- Natural Language Processing (NLP): Utilized by chatbots and virtual agents to understand, interpret, and respond to customer inquiries or requests in a human-like manner.
- Voice Recognition and Speech Analytics: Used for real-time call routing, voice authentication, or sentiment analysis to detect customer moods, identify customer needs, improve the quality of interactions, and enable effective call transfers.
- Predictive Analytics: Analyzes historical data to forecast call volumes, identify patterns, and optimize staffing levels to ensure adequate agent availability without resource wastage.
- Machine Learning and AI-based Recommendations: Analyzes customer data and call history to offer personalized recommendations or suggestions to agents, improving the overall customer experience.

Evaluate the capabilities, features, and limitations of each technology and match them with your defined objectives and requirements.

4.3 Consider Scalability and Compatibility

Assess the scalability of the AI technologies you are considering. Ensure that the selected solutions can accommodate the growth of your call center and its evolving needs. Consider vendor support and feedback, future development plans, and ensure that the AI tools are compatible with your existing call center infrastructure, software systems, and data management processes. Integration with existing systems such as CRM, ticketing, or knowledge base platforms is crucial for streamlining operations and delivering a seamless customer experience.

4.4 Evaluate Vendor Reputation and Support

Evaluate the reputation and track record of potential vendors of the technology. Look for providers with proven expertise, experience, and a solid customer base. Consider factors such as service level agreements, ongoing support, training, and future enhancements. Engage in discussions, demos, and pilot programs to assess how well the technology aligns with your call center's specific needs and workflows.

4.5 Cost-Benefit Analysis

Perform a thorough cost-benefit analysis to assess the value proposition of each AI technology. Consider the upfront costs, ongoing maintenance expenses, and potential integration costs. Weigh these against the benefits, such as improved efficiency, increased customer satisfaction, and reduced costs in the long run. Seek input from relevant stakeholders, including management, IT teams, and call center agents, to gain multiple perspectives on the potential return on investment.

4.6 Pilot Testing and Validation

Before implementing AI technologies on a larger scale, conduct pilot testing to validate their effectiveness. Select a small group of agents and customers to participate in the pilot program. Monitor KPIs, collect feedback, and evaluate the impact of the AI technologies on agent productivity, customer satisfaction, and overall call center performance. Make adjustments and refinements based on the learnings from the pilot phase.

4.7 Continuous Evaluation and Improvement

Once AI technologies are implemented, continuously evaluate their performance and impact. Track KPIs, monitor customer feedback, and gather insights to make data-driven decisions for ongoing improvements. Stay updated with advancements in AI technologies and emerging trends in the call center industry to assess future opportunities for enhancement.

Choosing the right AI technologies for you is a critical step in the call center transformation journey. By clearly defining your objectives, exploring available technologies, considering scalability and compatibility, evaluating vendor reputation and support, performing cost-benefit analysis, conducting pilot testing, and continuously evaluating and improving, you can select the AI tools that will enhance your call center operations and provide the best value for your organization. Careful consideration and selection of AI technologies will ensure a successful integration and help achieve the desired improvements in efficiency, customer experience, and overall call center performance.

Step 5: Implement AI technologies in a phased approach

To ensure a smooth transition and maximize the success of the AI integration, it is advisable to implement AI technologies in a phased approach rather than all at once. This phased implementation allows for testing, learning, and adjustments, as well as providing your staff with time to adapt to the changes. Here's how you can implement AI technologies in a phased manner:

5.1 Select Pilot Teams and Functions

Identify a small group of agents or teams, preferably those who are open to embracing new technologies, to participate in the pilot program. Choosing a diverse group representing different call types or customer segments will provide a comprehensive understanding of the AI technologies' effectiveness across various scenarios. Define specific functions or tasks that will be handled using AI technologies during the pilot phase.

5.2 Set Clear Objectives and KPIs

Establish clear objectives and KPIs for the pilot program. Align these objectives with the outcomes you wish to achieve, such as reducing average handle time or improving customer satisfaction. The KPIs should be measurable and specific, allowing you to track the effectiveness of the AI technologies and compare them against existing benchmarks.

5.3 Provide Training and Support

Before the pilot phase begins, provide comprehensive training to the participating agents and supervisors. Ensure they have a clear understanding of how AI technologies will be integrated into their workflows and how they can leverage these tools to enhance their performance. Offer ongoing support, documentation, and resources to help them navigate the new system and address any challenges that may arise.

5.4 Deploy and Monitor the Pilot Program

Implement the selected AI technologies for the designated pilot teams or functions. Monitor the performance closely during this phase and collect feedback from both agents and customers. Keep track of the KPIs established for the pilot and evaluate the impact of the AI technologies. Regularly communicate with the pilot participants to gather insights, identify areas for improvement, and address any concerns or issues that may arise.

5.5 Refine and Adjust

Based on the feedback and performance during the pilot program, make necessary adjustments and refinements to optimize the AI technologies for your call center environment. This may include tweaking the algorithms, modifying workflows, or improving the training materials. Consider involving pilot participants in the refinement process to gather their input and insights.

5.6 Gradual Rollout

Once you have validated the performance and effectiveness of the AI technologies through the pilot program, gradually roll out the technologies to additional teams or functions within your call center. Monitor the performance and impact of the expanded implementation, and make any necessary adjustments as you scale up.

5.7 Continuous Monitoring and Feedback

Continuously monitor the performance of the AI technologies as they are being rolled out across the call center. Collect ongoing feedback from agents, supervisors, and customers to understand their experience and identify areas for further improvement. Monitor the KPIs established in Step 1 and compare them against the initial baseline to measure the impact and success of the AI implementation.

Implementing AI technologies in a phased approach allows for a smooth transition, provides opportunities for learning and adjustments, and enables your staff to adapt to the changes gradually. Starting with a pilot program, setting clear objectives and KPIs, providing training and support, monitoring performance, refining and adjusting, and gradually rolling out the technologies across your call center will help ensure a successful integration. Continuous monitoring, feedback, and improvement will ultimately contribute to an AI-powered call center that delivers enhanced efficiency, improved customer experience, and increased agent productivity.

Step 6: Provide training and support for employees

As your call center undergoes the transformation and integrates AI technologies, providing comprehensive training and support to your employees is crucial for their successful adoption and utilization of these tools. Here are key aspects to consider when designing training and support programs for your staff:

6.1 Develop Training Materials

Create comprehensive training materials that cover both the theoretical and practical aspects of using AI technologies in the call center. These materials should include step-by-step guides, best practices, and real-life examples to illustrate how AI tools can enhance productivity and customer interactions. Ensure that the training materials are accessible and easily understandable for all employees, regardless of their technical proficiency.

6.2 Emphasize the Importance of Human Touch

During the training sessions, emphasize the value of maintaining a human touch in customer interactions, even with the integration of AI technologies. Highlight that AI tools are meant to assist agents, not replace them. Reinforce the importance of empathy, active listening, and problem-solving skills in delivering exceptional customer experiences. Help agents understand how AI technologies can free up their time from mundane tasks, enabling them to focus on building relationships and providing personalized assistance to customers.

6.3 Address Concerns and Misconceptions

Recognize that employees may have concerns or misconceptions about the integration of AI technologies. Schedule open discussions or Q&A sessions to address these concerns and provide clarifications. Address any fears or uncertainties they may have about their job security or the impact of AI on their roles. Clearly communicate that AI is intended to enhance their performance and efficiency rather than replace them. Offer reassurance and highlight the benefits of AI technologies in simplifying their workflows and improving customer satisfaction.

6.4 Hands-On Training and Simulations

Provide hands-on training that allows employees to practice using various AI tools in simulated scenarios. This approach helps build confidence, familiarity, and competence in using the technologies effectively. Conduct role-playing exercises to simulate real interactions with customers and guide employees on how to leverage AI tools to deliver efficient and empathetic service.

6.5 Continuous Monitoring and Feedback

Implement a system for continuous monitoring and feedback, where supervisors and team leaders regularly assess the use of AI technologies by agents. Provide constructive feedback to help employees improve their utilization of AI tools and reinforce positive practices. Use coaching and mentoring sessions to address areas for improvement and share success stories to motivate and inspire the team.

6.6 Foster a Culture of Learning and Adaptation

Encourage a culture of continuous learning and adaptation as AI technologies evolve and new updates are introduced. Organize regular training sessions to keep employees updated with the latest features and functionalities of the AI tools. Provide ongoing support, including dedicated helpdesk resources or knowledge bases, where employees can access information, troubleshoot issues, or seek guidance on using the AI technologies effectively.

6.7 Celebrate Successes

Recognize and celebrate the successes and achievements of employees as they embrace and utilize AI technologies. Acknowledge individuals or teams who demonstrate outstanding performance in integrating AI into their workflows and achieving positive outcomes. This recognition will encourage others to embrace the changes and foster a positive mindset towards AI technologies.

Providing comprehensive training and support for your employees is essential to ensure the successful adoption and utilization of AI technologies in the call center. By emphasizing the importance of the human touch, addressing concerns and misconceptions, providing hands-on training, continuous monitoring and feedback, fostering a culture of learning, and celebrating successes, you can empower your staff to leverage AI tools effectively, enhance their productivity, and deliver exceptional customer experiences. Remember, the combination of AI technology and human expertise can create a strong partnership that elevates your call center to new heights.

Step 7: Monitor performance and iterate

Monitoring the performance of your transformed call center is crucial to ensuring the ongoing success of your AI integration efforts. When you regularly analyze key performance indicators (KPIs), customer feedback, and agent performance metrics, you gain valuable insights into how well the AI technologies are performing and make necessary adjustments or improvements. Follow these steps to effectively monitor performance and iterate on your AI strategies:

7.1 Establish Key Performance Indicators (KPIs)

Define a set of KPIs that align with your call center objectives and measure the effectiveness of the AI technologies. These KPIs could include metrics such as average handle time, first-call resolution rate, customer satisfaction score, agent productivity, and cost-per-contact. Ensure that these KPIs are measurable, relevant, and aligned with your call center's goals (see Step 1 above).

7.2 Collect and Analyze Data

Regularly collect and analyze data related to the identified KPIs. These data can come from various sources, including call center software analytics, customer feedback surveys, quality monitoring tools, and performance management systems. Leverage data visualization tools and reporting dashboards to gain actionable insights and identify trends or patterns that impact performance.

7.3 Identify Areas for Improvement

Based on the analysis of the collected data, identify areas for improvement where the AI technologies may not be performing optimally or where there is room for enhancement. Look for recurring issues, bottlenecks, or opportunities for efficiency gains. Consider both quantitative data (e.g., KPI metrics) and qualitative data (e.g., customer feedback) to gain a holistic understanding of performance.

7.4 Seek Customer Feedback

Regularly collect customer feedback through surveys, feedback forms, or other channels to gauge their satisfaction with the interactions handled by AI technologies. Analyze this feedback to identify areas where the AI technologies may not be meeting customer expectations or where the human touch may be required. Take note of any pain points or friction points mentioned by customers and address them in your iterations.

7.5 Involve Employees in the Process

Include your call center agents and supervisors in the performance monitoring process. Seek their input on the effectiveness of the AI technologies and gather insights from their day-to-day experiences. Conduct regular debrief sessions, team meetings, or one-on-one discussions to understand any challenges or opportunities they have identified. Their firsthand knowledge can provide valuable insights for improvement.

7.6 Make Iterative Adjustments:

Based on the insights gained from KPI analysis, customer feedback, and employee input, make iterative adjustments to your AI strategies. This could involve refining the AI algorithms, improving the training provided to agents, enhancing the integration between AI tools and existing systems, or revisiting the design and functionality of chatbots or virtual agents. Continuously evaluate the impact of any changes made and iterate further as needed.

7.7 Evaluate Long-Term Performance

Regularly assess the long-term performance of your transformed call center to ensure that the AI technologies are delivering your desired outcomes. Track the progress of the identified KPIs over time and compare them against the baseline you established at the beginning of the transformation process. Identify trends, patterns, or areas for improvement that may require additional attention or fine-tuning.

Monitoring the performance of your transformed call center on an ongoing basis is essential to ensure that the AI technologies are delivering the expected results. By analyzing KPIs, soliciting customer feedback, involving employees in the process, and making iterative adjustments based on insights gained, you can continuously improve the performance, efficiency, and customer satisfaction of your call center. Remember that the transformation process is not a one-time event but an ongoing journey that requires vigilance, adaptability, and a commitment to delivering exceptional customer experiences.

Conclusion

Transforming your call center using AI technologies is an exciting opportunity to revolutionize your operations, significantly improve customer service, and optimize costs. By following the steps outlined in this project plan, you can successfully navigate the transformation process while keeping the human touch intact.

By defining clear objectives and establishing measurable KPIs, you set the foundation for success and ensure that the AI integration aligns with your business goals. Assessing your current call center operations helps you identify pain points and areas for improvement, as well as determine where AI can enhance existing processes.

Developing a roadmap for AI integration allows for a systematic and phased approach to implementation, starting with low-risk and high-value use cases. Selecting the right AI technologies, and considering scalability and compatibility, ensures that your chosen tools align with your objectives and seamlessly integrate into your existing systems.

Providing comprehensive training and support to your employees is crucial to their successful adoption of AI technologies. Emphasize the importance of the human touch in customer interactions and address any concerns or misconceptions they may have. Continuous monitoring and feedback, coupled with coaching and mentoring, will help build a strong human-AI partnership.

Monitoring performance using KPIs, analyzing customer feedback, and evaluating agent performance metrics enable you to gather insights and make necessary adjustments to ensure ongoing success. Remember to involve your employees in the process and celebrate successes along the way.

In conclusion, the call center of the future is not about replacing human interaction but leveraging AI as a powerful ally to empower your agents to deliver exceptional customer experiences. Embrace the transformative power of AI technologies, with its potential to streamline operations, enhance customer service, and optimize costs. To guide you through this journey, consider working with AI Architects who specialize in call center transformations and can provide the expertise and guidance needed for a successful integration. Embrace the future of call centers and unlock the full potential of AI technologies to revolutionize your customer interactions and drive your business forward.

Transforming the CPG Industry with AI

Introduction

Consumer Packaged Goods (CPG) companies are constantly seeking ways to improve efficiencies, increase revenue, and reduce costs to maintain their competitive edge in today's fast-paced market. In recent years, the advent of Artificial Intelligence (AI) has opened up unprecedented opportunities for CPG companies to revolutionize their operations. By leveraging AI technologies, CPG companies can unlock new levels of efficiency, enhance decision-making processes, and create a more sustainable future. In this chapter, we will delve into the various ways that AI can transform the CPG industry and enable companies to thrive in an increasingly dynamic landscape.

Optimizing Supply Chain Management

Supply chain management is a complex process that involves the coordination of various activities, from procurement and production to distribution and customer service. CPG companies operate in a highly dynamic market with ever-changing consumer demands and evolving market trends. This uncertainty often leads to challenges in managing inventory levels effectively and meeting customer expectations.

By leveraging AI-powered solutions, you can gain a competitive edge by optimizing your supply chain management processes. AI algorithms have the ability to analyze vast volumes of data, such as historical sales data, customer behavior patterns, and market trends, to forecast demand accurately. These algorithms take into account factors like seasonality, promotions, and even external factors like weather patterns or economic indicators.

With accurate demand forecasting, CPG companies can make informed decisions regarding inventory levels and production schedules. By reducing stock-outs and minimizing excess inventory, you can optimize storage space, reduce waste, and avoid high carrying costs. Additionally, AI algorithms can dynamically adjust inventory levels based on real-time sales data, ensuring that products are available at the right time and place, thus enhancing customer satisfaction.

Moreover, AI-powered solutions can significantly improve logistics efficiency. With real-time data analysis, CPG companies can optimize transportation routes, ensuring faster and more cost-effective delivery. AI algorithms can take into consideration factors like traffic conditions, fuel costs, and delivery prioritization, enabling you to make intelligent decisions that minimize transportation costs while maximizing service levels.

Another key aspect of supply chain management is supplier management. AI solutions can aid in identifying and selecting the right suppliers for you, based on factors such as quality, lead time, and cost. By evaluating large datasets and conducting supplier performance analysis, you can ensure a reliable supply of high-quality raw materials while minimizing supply chain disruptions.

Furthermore, AI can enhance visibility in the supply chain by integrating data from various systems and providing real-time insights into the status of orders, inventory levels, and production schedules. This transparency allows you to proactively identify bottlenecks, prioritize tasks, and reduce delays, resulting in improved overall operational efficiency.

In addition to optimizing existing supply chain processes, AI can also enable CPG companies to explore new possibilities for innovation. By analyzing consumer data and market trends, AI algorithms can identify emerging customer preferences, allowing you to adjust your product offerings accordingly. AI can also assist in identifying new market opportunities, developing innovative products, and creating more targeted marketing strategies to capture consumers' attention.

Overall, integrating AI-powered solutions into supply chain management processes can revolutionize the way CPG companies operate. You can reduce costs, improve customer satisfaction, and gain a competitive advantage by accurately forecasting demand, optimizing inventory levels, enhancing logistics efficiency, and utilizing real-time data insights.. Embracing AI technology is therefore essential for CPG companies who want to thrive in a fast-paced and volatile consumer goods industry. It ensures you stay ahead of the curve and continue to meet the evolving demands of modern consumers.

Personalized Marketing and Customer Experience

Personalized marketing has become a crucial aspect of successful CPG companies' strategies. Traditional mass marketing approaches may no longer suffice when consumers expect tailored experiences and individualized recommendations. AI technologies offer you the ability to leverage customer data and create personalized marketing campaigns that resonate with each consumer uniquely.

AI-powered algorithms can analyze vast consumer data, including purchase history, browsing behavior, social media interactions, and demographic information. CPG companies can gain a deeper understanding of their customers and their preferences by extracting meaningful insights from these data. Machine learning algorithms can identify patterns and correlations within the data, enabling you to make accurate predictions about individual purchasing behaviors or preferences.

This level of personalization allows CPG companies to deliver targeted product recommendations to consumers. Through personalized recommendations, customers are more likely to find products that align with their needs and preferences, increasing the chances of conversion and repeat purchases. As a result, you can build stronger customer relationships and enhance customer loyalty.

AI technology also enables CPG companies to create highly targeted advertisements. By analyzing consumer data, AI algorithms can identify specific attributes, interests, or behaviors that make a consumer more likely to respond positively to an ad. This allows you to deliver relevant and engaging advertisements to the right audience, enhancing the effectiveness of your marketing campaigns and increasing the conversion rate.

Furthermore, AI-powered chatbots and virtual assistants can provide personalized customer support, answering product-related inquiries, providing recommendations, and resolving issues in real-time. Natural language processing algorithms enable these AI systems to understand and respond to customer inquiries accurately and efficiently. This not only improves the customer experience but also saves time and resources for you by automating routine customer support tasks.

CPG companies can also leverage AI to create personalized promotions and offers. By analyzing customer data, AI algorithms can identify specific customer segments or individual preferences that can be targeted with tailored promotions. This allows you to offer discounts, coupons, or exclusive offers that are highly relevant to individual customers, increasing the likelihood of conversion and repeat purchases.

By applying AI technologies to personalized marketing, CPG companies can achieve several advantages. First and foremost, the technology can create more meaningful and relevant experiences for their customers, fostering stronger connections and brand loyalty – customers are more likely to engage with personalized content and recommendations, which leads to increased sales and revenue for the company.

Furthermore, personalized marketing allows you to optimize your marketing spend. Instead of deploying blanket marketing campaigns with a wide reach but potentially lower conversion rates, AI enables companies to target specific customer segments or individuals with higher precision, ensuring that marketing efforts are directed where they will yield the best outcomes. This results in a more efficient allocation of resources and a higher return on investment.

Leveraging AI technologies for personalized marketing and customer experience in the CPG industry has immense potential. AI algorithms that analyze consumer data enable you to deliver targeted recommendations, create personalized advertisements, provide real-time customer support, and offer tailored promotions. This level of personalization enhances customer satisfaction, increases brand loyalty, and drives revenue growth for CPG companies. Embracing AI-powered personalization is a key differentiator in a competitive market and a way for companies to connect with customers on a deeper level in the digital age.

Quality Control and Product Innovation

Ensuring product quality is paramount for CPG companies. AI-powered technologies can play a crucial role in automating quality control processes, enhancing efficiency, and minimizing errors in the production line.

For example, computer vision, a key application of AI, utilizes algorithms to analyze visual data and identify defects or inconsistencies in products. By integrating AI-powered vision systems into the production line, CPG companies can perform real-time inspections, identifying defects that may go unnoticed by human operators. This automated approach not only increases the speed of inspections but also improves accuracy and consistency in identifying and rejecting faulty products. By preventing defective products from reaching the market, CPG companies can safeguard their brand reputation and minimize the risk of customer complaints or returns.

Moreover, AI-driven quality control systems can continuously learn and adapt. By analyzing large volumes of historical product data, images, and inspection results, AI algorithms can fine-tune their detection capabilities to identify even the most subtle defects. This adaptive learning capability allows the system to become increasingly accurate over time, enabling companies to continuously improve their quality control processes.

In addition to automating quality control, AI can also drive product innovation. You can leverage data analytics and AI techniques to extract valuable insights from multiple sources, including consumer feedback, social media trends, online reviews, and market data. AI algorithms can identify patterns, sentiments, and emerging preferences, helping you understand customer needs better and identify potential gaps or opportunities in their product offerings.

By analyzing customer feedback, AI can identify common complaints, issues, or desired improvements, which can then be incorporated into the product development process. This proactive approach enables CPG companies to address customer concerns, iterate on existing products, and enhance product performance – ensuring that customers receive products that meet their evolving expectations.

Additionally, AI can assist in identifying emerging trends or market niches that you can tap into for innovative product development. By analyzing social media conversations, purchasing behavior, and market data, AI algorithms can uncover hidden insights and potential market demands that may not be readily apparent. This intelligence can guide product innovation efforts, enabling you to develop new products or variants that resonate with current or emerging consumer preferences.

AI algorithms can also analyze and optimize formulation and recipe data, which leads to improved product consistency and sensory attributes. By leveraging machine learning models, you can identify optimal ingredient combinations and processing parameters, reducing variability and enhancing the overall quality of your products.

Overall, AI technologies offer significant advantages for quality control and product innovation in the CPG industry. By automating quality control processes with computer vision, companies can improve efficiency, accuracy, and consistency in detecting product defects. AI-driven analysis of consumer feedback, market trends, and data insights can inform product development efforts, leading to enhanced customer satisfaction and greater innovation. And by leveraging AI in quality control and product innovation, you can ensure consistently high-quality products that meet customer expectations and remain competitive in the market.

Forecasting and Demand Planning

Demand forecasting and planning form the backbone of successful inventory management for CPG companies. The integration of AI solutions into these processes can revolutionize the accuracy and efficiency of forecasting, and allow you to optimize inventory levels and respond swiftly to changes in consumer demand.

AI algorithms have the ability to analyze vast amounts of historical sales data, market trends, and external factors that influence demand. By leveraging these data – and the lagging and leading indicators within the data – CPG companies can gain valuable insights into patterns, seasonality, and other factors that impact demand fluctuations. AI algorithms can identify correlations and trends within the data, enabling accurate predictions of future demand.

With AI-powered demand forecasting, CPG companies can dynamically adjust their forecasts in real-time based on relevant factors such as promotions, pricing changes, or emerging market trends. This flexibility allows you to respond promptly to shifts in demand, ensuring that inventory levels are appropriately adjusted to meet consumer needs. By accurately predicting demand, you can reduce stockouts, avoid excess inventory, and allocate resources more effectively, leading to improved supply chain efficiency.

Another advantage of AI-driven demand planning is its ability to incorporate external factors that can influence demand patterns. For example, AI algorithms can integrate data on weather patterns to anticipate changes in demand for seasonal or weather-dependent products. By considering socio-economic factors, such as economic indicators or population changes, AI can further refine demand forecasts, helping CPG companies adapt to market conditions.

Moreover, AI-powered demand planning tools can optimize inventory levels by automatically adjusting forecasts and recommending reorder points. This automation eliminates the need for manual calculations and reduces the risk of human error. By maintaining optimal inventory levels, you can minimize carrying costs, reduce wastage, and free up valuable storage space.

Furthermore, AI-powered demand planning tools can optimize production schedules and procurement processes. By aligning production and procurement with demand forecasts, companies can avoid production bottlenecks, reduce lead times, and ensure a seamless flow of inventory. This increased efficiency decreases the risk of stockouts and minimizes excess inventory that could lead to capital tied up in unutilized resources.

Another advantage of integrating AI into demand planning it that it enables you to enhance sales performance. By accurately forecasting demand, you can proactively allocate resources, target promotions, and adjust pricing strategies based on expected demand fluctuations. This proactive approach improves the accuracy of sales forecasting and enables you to optimize pricing and promotional strategies to drive revenue growth.

Furthermore, AI algorithms can identify demand patterns and trends that may not be immediately apparent to human planners. By analyzing customer preferences, purchase patterns, and market data, AI algorithms can not only uncover latent demand, but identify emerging market segments and guide you in developing targeted marketing campaigns and product innovations.

Overall, AI-powered demand forecasting and planning are invaluable tools for CPG companies. By leveraging AI algorithms to analyze historical data, market trends, and external factors, you can accurately forecast demand, optimize inventory levels, and improve your supply chain efficiency. Through improved demand planning, you can reduce stockouts, minimize excess inventory, enhance sales performance, and drive revenue growth. Embracing AI in demand forecasting and planning is therefore a significant step for CPG companies to optimize their operations and stay ahead in a rapidly evolving marketplace.

Enhancing Manufacturing Efficiency

Manufacturing efficiency is a critical factor in the success of CPG companies. AI technologies offer tremendous opportunities to enhance operational efficiency and reduce downtime, ultimately leading to cost savings and improved productivity.

By leveraging machine learning algorithms, CPG companies can analyze vast amounts of data collected from sensors, equipment, and historical production records. These AI algorithms can identify patterns, correlations, and anomalies in the data, enabling you to optimize production parameters and fine-tune your manufacturing processes.

One way AI can enhance manufacturing efficiency is through the optimization of production parameters. By analyzing data collected from sensors and historical production records, AI algorithms can identify optimal settings for variables such as temperature, pressure, speed, or ingredient quantities. These algorithms continuously learn from data, adjusting the parameters in real-time to achieve higher product quality, reduce waste, and improve overall efficiency. When you optimize production parameters, you increase output, minimize defects, and reduce energy consumption.

Another aspect where AI technologies excel is in preventative maintenance. By analyzing sensor data and historical maintenance records, AI algorithms can predict the likelihood of equipment failures and recommend preventative maintenance schedules. This proactive approach allows companies to address potential issues before they cause unplanned downtime, reducing production disruptions and minimizing the cost of repairs. By optimizing maintenance schedules, CPG companies can therefore extend the lifespan of their equipment and enhance overall operational efficiency.

Predictive analytics is another AI-powered tool that can significantly enhance manufacturing efficiency. By analyzing data from various sources, such as sensor readings, historical records, and vendor experience, AI algorithms can predict potential equipment failures and detect deviations from production targets. This early detection enables companies to take corrective actions promptly, preventing downtime and minimizing the impact on production schedules. Predictive analytics can also assist in improving equipment effectiveness metrics, such as overall equipment effectiveness (OEE), by identifying areas for improvement and optimizing the utilization of resources.

Furthermore, AI technologies can automate data collection and analysis, reducing the reliance on manual labor and the potential for human error. When CPG companies integrate AI-powered systems with production lines, they can collect real-time data, monitor performance, and identify bottlenecks or inefficiencies more effectively. This automated data analysis allows for faster decision-making and provides actionable insights for process improvement.

AI technologies can also facilitate the implementation of smart manufacturing, where machinery and systems communicate and cooperate in real-time. Utilizing AI algorithms to analyze data collected from interconnected sensors and equipment, means CPG companies can achieve seamless coordination and optimization of production processes. This level of automation and synchronization leads to improved throughput, reduced cycle time, and increased overall manufacturing efficiency.

AI technologies have the potential to revolutionize manufacturing efficiency in the CPG industry. By optimizing production parameters, enabling preventative maintenance, utilizing predictive analytics, automating data collection and analysis, and facilitating smart manufacturing, CPG companies can achieve significant improvements in operational efficiency. Through reduced downtime, increased productivity, and cost savings, AI technologies provide you with a competitive edge in the market, allowing you to meet customer demands efficiently and maintain a lead in the industry.

Conclusion

In conclusion, the integration of AI in the CPG industry has the potential to revolutionize operations and drive success. The various ways that AI can be leveraged in the CPG space, as discussed throughout this chapter, highlight the immense benefits it offers.

By optimizing supply chain management through AI-powered solutions, CPG companies can streamline operations, forecast demand accurately, and reduce costs. This results in improved inventory management, enhanced logistics efficiency, and increased customer satisfaction. Personalized marketing and customer experience, made possible by AI technologies, allow companies to engage customers on a deeper level, driving sales and fostering customer loyalty.

The automation and accuracy of AI-powered quality control processes ensure consistent product quality and safeguard brand reputation. AI-driven analysis of consumer feedback, social media trends, and market data empowers CPG companies to identify gaps in product offerings, driving innovation and enhancing their competitiveness in the market.

AI's ability to forecast demand accurately and optimize product planning enables CPG companies to prevent stockouts and minimize excess inventory. This results in improved supply chain efficiency, reduced wastage, and optimized storage costs. Furthermore, AI technologies enhance manufacturing efficiency by optimizing production parameters, facilitating preventative maintenance, and utilizing predictive analytics to reduce downtime and increase productivity.

In a rapidly evolving marketplace, embracing AI is no longer an option but a necessity for CPG companies seeking sustainable success. AI offers unparalleled opportunities to drive efficiencies, enhance revenue generation, and reduce costs throughout the entire value chain. By partnering with AI Architects, CPG companies can harness the full potential of AI in their operations and gain a competitive advantage in the dynamic CPG market.

How AI Empowers Professional Services Firms

Introduction

IN AN ERA DRIVEN BY UNPRECEDENTED TECHNOLOGICAL PROGRESS, it comes as no surprise that artificial intelligence (AI) has emerged as a game-changer across industries. The professional services sector, encompassing management consulting, legal services, financial advisory, and more, stands to benefit significantly from AI's transformative capabilities. By harnessing AI, professional services firms have the opportunity to unlock unprecedented potential, empowering their consultants to be more effective in serving their clients. This chapter explores the manifold ways in which AI can revolutionize the professional services landscape and elevate client satisfaction.

Augmenting Consultant Expertise

One of the primary advantages of AI lies in its capacity to augment human expertise, enabling consultants to make more informed decisions and provide better quality advice. Through advanced predictive analytics, machine learning algorithms, and natural language processing techniques, AI can analyze vast amounts of data to identify patterns, uncover insights, and make recommendations that are traditionally time-consuming or impractical for humans to achieve alone.

Data Analysis and Insights

AI-powered tools have the remarkable capability to handle vast amounts of data, extracting valuable insights and patterns that would be arduous or time-consuming for humans to accomplish alone. By leveraging predictive analytics, machine learning algorithms, and natural language processing techniques, AI can quickly analyze complex datasets and present consultants with actionable insights. Armed with this information, consultants are empowered to make more informed recommendations to clients. For instance, AI can identify market trends, customer preferences, and potential risks, enabling clients to capitalize on new business opportunities while proactively mitigating potential threats. By uncovering these critical insights, consultants equipped with AI can optimize strategies, set realistic goals, and drive better outcomes for their clients.

Expert Knowledge Repositories

In addition to data analysis, AI enables the development of comprehensive knowledge management systems that serve as centralized repositories of institutional knowledge. These AI-driven systems encompass an array of tools and technologies that enhance the accessibility and usability of information for consultants. By utilizing AI algorithms, these knowledge repositories can organize vast collections of past case studies, research papers, best practices, and industry benchmarks. Such repositories enable consultants to instantaneously access relevant information, saving time and effort in their research endeavors. Moreover, AI-driven knowledge management systems foster collaboration among consultants, facilitating the exchange of expertise and leading to higher-quality client deliverables. By consolidating and leveraging the collective knowledge within an organization, consultants armed with AI can offer best-in-class solutions based on the experiences and successes of their colleagues, thereby elevating the overall quality of their client services.

AI's ability to augment consultants' expertise through data analysis and insights, as well as the establishment of expert knowledge repositories, revolutionizes the way professional services firms engage with clients. By leveraging these AI capabilities, consultants are equipped with a deeper understanding of their clients' needs and a stronger foundation of knowledge, empowering them to provide better advice, drive innovation, and achieve remarkable client outcomes.

Enhanced Accuracy and Efficiency

AI has the potential to revolutionize the way professional services firms operate, reducing mundane manual tasks, eliminating human error, and significantly enhancing overall efficiency.

Process Automation

AI-driven process automation holds immense potential for professional services firms to optimize their operations and enhance overall efficiency.

Mundane, repetitive tasks such as data entry, report generation, and contract management can be automated using AI technology. By leveraging machine learning algorithms and robotic process automation (RPA), organizations can streamline these time-consuming activities, significantly reducing the risk of human error and freeing up valuable consultant time. As a result, consultants can focus their efforts on more strategic and high-value activities, such as in-depth analysis, strategy development, and client interactions. With these routine tasks automated, professional services firms can deliver exceptional client service while simultaneously optimizing their internal resource allocation and maximizing productivity.

Legal and Compliance Support

The legal sector is one specific area within professional services where AI can have a profound impact. AI-powered tools can analyze extensive legal databases, providing comprehensive legal support to consultants. For instance, AI algorithms can perform due diligence exercises by swiftly analyzing large volumes of legal documents, highlighting key aspects, and identifying potential risks. This capability significantly expedites the contract review process, saving valuable time while ensuring thoroughness and accuracy. Natural language processing (NLP) and machine translation further enhance AI's capabilities in the legal field. These technologies can interpret legal text, extracting insights from complex and nuanced legal documents, statutes, and regulations. By leveraging AI for legal and compliance support, professional services firms can enhance their efficiency, mitigate risks, and provide clients with comprehensive and accurate legal counsel.

The enhanced accuracy and efficiency brought about by AI in professional services firms have far-reaching benefits. By automating mundane tasks and streamlining operations, firms can optimize their resources, reduce errors, and improve overall productivity. Additionally, AI-powered tools in the legal sector offer invaluable support, enabling comprehensive due diligence and enhancing speed and accuracy in legal document analysis. Leveraging AI technology in these ways allows professional services firms to not only enhance their competitive advantage, but also deliver exceptional client service, focusing their expertise on high-value activities that drive success.

Personalized Client Engagement

AI has the potential to revolutionize client interactions and drive personalized experiences by leveraging data and cognitive capabilities.

Client Profiling and Segmentation

AI's ability to assimilate, process, and analyze vast amounts of client data from various sources opens up opportunities for consultants to develop comprehensive client profiles and segmentation strategies. Through AI-driven analytics, consultants can gain deeper insights into clients' needs, preferences, and behaviors, allowing for a more personalized approach to client engagement. By analyzing transactional data, social media activity, customer feedback, and other relevant sources, AI algorithms can identify patterns, trends, and correlations to create nuanced portraits of individual clients and client segments. Armed with this knowledge, consultants can tailor their services, recommendations, and strategies to meet their clients' specific requirements. This personalized approach fosters stronger client relationships, builds trust, and enhances overall client satisfaction.

Virtual Assistants

Intelligent virtual assistants and chatbots powered by AI have emerged as valuable tools in client engagement. These virtual assistants can handle routine and repetitive tasks, instantly responding to commonly asked questions, capturing client preferences, and managing administrative tasks, such as scheduling appointments. By leveraging natural language processing and machine learning, virtual assistants can simulate human-like conversations and provide accurate and timely information to clients. This automation of basic interactions allows consultants to focus their time and expertise on more intricate, complex, and high-value discussions with clients. Virtual assistants not only enhance the efficiency of client engagement but also contribute to a seamless and personalized client experience by providing 24/7 support and immediate response capabilities. The combination of AI-powered virtual assistants and human consultants creates a synergistic approach, ensuring that the best expertise and personalized attention are offered to clients throughout their journey.

AI enables this kind of personalized client engagement by leveraging data insights and cognitive capabilities. Through client profiling and segmentation, consultants can leverage AI's analytical power to gain a deeper understanding of client needs, preferences, and behaviors. This knowledge leads to customized services, recommendations, and strategies that align with individual client requirements. Additionally, virtual assistants powered by AI automate routine tasks, provide instant responses, and capture client preferences, enhancing the overall client experience while freeing up consultants' time to focus on higher-value interactions. By harnessing AI for personalized client engagement, professional services firms can strengthen client relationships, improve satisfaction, and become trusted advisors in delivering tailored solutions.

Dynamic Pricing and Revenue Optimization

AI can be instrumental in optimizing pricing strategies and revenue management for professional services firms, enabling them to maximize profitability while delighting clients.

Pricing Optimization

AI holds immense potential for professional services firms to optimize their pricing strategies, ensuring that they are competitive, profitable, and aligned with market dynamics. When they leverage AI-powered algorithms, firms can analyze a wide range of data sources, including market trends, competitors' pricing strategies, historical data, customer behavior, and more. With this comprehensive analysis, AI algorithms can recommend optimal pricing structures that balance profitability and client value. Moreover, AI can continuously monitor and adapt pricing strategies in real-time to respond to market changes, demand fluctuations, or competitive moves. By leveraging AI for pricing optimization, firms can avoid revenue leakage, capture untapped opportunities, and ensure that their pricing strategies are dynamic, data-driven, and tailored to maximize profitability while impressing clients with fair and competitive pricing.

Dynamic Resource Allocation

Optimizing resource allocation is another area where AI can significantly enhance profitability and client satisfaction. AI algorithms can analyze historical data, project future demand patterns, and account for variations in client needs and project requirements. By leveraging these insights, firms can optimize consultant staffing levels, ensuring that the right expertise is allocated to the right projects at the right time. AI-driven resource allocation can minimize resource bottlenecks, avoid overstaffing or understaffing, and maximize billable hours. This efficiency not only improves profitability but also results in better utilization of consultants' expertise. By matching consultants' skills with project requirements, firms can deliver high-quality services, enhance client satisfaction, and establish a reputation for personalized and effective resource allocation. AI's predictive capabilities in dynamic resource allocation enable firms to not only proactively adapt their operations but also optimize project delivery and effectively manage capacity to achieve optimal revenue generation.

In summary, AI's efficiency in refining pricing strategies and dynamically allocating resources offers significant advantages to professional services firms. By leveraging AI algorithms for pricing improvements, firms can ensure competitive pricing, maximize profitability, and capture market opportunities. Additionally, AI-driven resource allocation enables firms to fine-tune consultant staffing levels, reduce resource bottlenecks, and enhance client satisfaction by delivering high-quality services matched with clients' needs. Embracing AI for dynamic pricing and resource management empowers professional services firms to achieve better financial outcomes while providing enhanced value and client satisfaction.

Conclusion

The transformational power of AI presents an unprecedented opportunity for professional services firms to elevate their capabilities and deliver exceptional value to clients. By harnessing AI, firms can amplify their consultants' expertise, enhance accuracy and efficiency, personalize client engagement, and optimize pricing strategies. Embracing AI-driven technologies is not a choice but a necessity for professional services organizations to remain competitive and relevant in an ever-evolving industry.

By augmenting consultant expertise, AI empowers professionals to make more informed decisions and provide better quality advice through advanced data analysis and insights. The ability to process vast amounts of data enables consultants to uncover hidden patterns, identify opportunities, and mitigate risks, ultimately driving tangible business outcomes for their clients. Furthermore, AI-powered expert knowledge repositories promote collaboration among consultants and unlock collective institutional knowledge, raising the bar on client deliverables and driving innovation in service offerings.

The enhanced accuracy and efficiency offered by AI automation streamlines routine tasks, minimizing human error and freeing up consultants' time for more strategic and high-value activities. In the legal sector, AI-powered tools ensure comprehensive due diligence, contract analysis, and compliance reviews, enabling consultants to provide thorough and accurate legal counsel. This level of automation and precision optimizes operations, improves productivity, and enables firms to provide a higher caliber of client service.

Moreover, AI-driven personalization revolutionizes client engagement by tailoring services to individual needs. With AI-powered client profiling and segmentation, consultants gain deeper insights into client preferences, enabling customized recommendations and strategies. Intelligent virtual assistants and chatbots enhance the client experience by providing instantaneous responses, capturing client preferences, and offering 24/7 support. This personalized approach builds stronger client relationships, fosters trust, and enhances overall satisfaction.

Furthermore, embracing AI for dynamic pricing and resource optimization provides a competitive advantage for professional services firms. AI-powered algorithms analyze market dynamics, competitors' pricing strategies, and historical data, enabling firms to maximize profitability while avoiding revenue leakage. By optimizing resource allocation based on AI-predicted demand patterns, firms can efficiently deploy consultants, maximize billable hours, and ensure high client satisfaction.

To lead in the era of AI-powered professional services, it is imperative for organizations to act now. Embracing AI requires a strategic approach, collaboration with AI Architects, and a commitment to cultural transformation. Professional services firms must invest in AI capabilities, develop data-driven strategies, and provide the necessary resources and training for consultants to leverage AI effectively.

The integration of AI into professional services firms not only enhances consultant expertise and operational efficiency but also enables personalized client engagement and dynamic pricing strategies. Those who embrace AI's transformative potential will be well-positioned for success in an era where data and technology drive business decisions. It is time for professional services firms to take decisive action, partner with AI architects, and embark on the journey toward becoming AI-powered organizations that deliver unparalleled client value.

Leveraging AI: Unlocking the Power of Inventory Management

Introduction

IN TODAY'S HIGHLY COMPETITIVE MARKET, organizations cannot afford to rely on outdated manual inventory management methods. These traditional approaches are not only time-consuming but also prone to errors due to human limitations. Additionally, they struggle to tap into the wealth of data available that could provide valuable insights for optimizing inventory control. This is where the integration of Artificial Intelligence (AI) into inventory management processes has proven to be a game-changer.

AI empowers businesses with sophisticated algorithms and machine learning capabilities, enabling them to make data-driven decisions, automate processes, and achieve higher levels of efficiency and accuracy. By leveraging the power of AI in inventory management, organizations can streamline supply chain operations, reduce costs, enhance customer satisfaction, and stay ahead of the competition.

Let's explore some of the key benefits that AI can bring to inventory management:

Demand Forecasting

Demand forecasting is a critical aspect of effective inventory management. Accurate predictions of future demand allow organizations to optimize inventory levels, minimize stock-outs, and reduce excess inventory. This is where AI-powered systems excel, utilizing advanced algorithms to analyze a vast array of data sources and generate highly accurate demand forecasts.

One notable example of AI-driven demand forecasting is Amazon. With its tremendous scale and vast product assortment, Amazon relies heavily on

AI and machine learning to manage its inventory. By analyzing historical sales data, customer browsing behavior, purchase patterns, and even external factors like weather patterns and social media sentiments, Amazon's AI-powered system can predict future demand with remarkable accuracy.

For instance, during holiday seasons or special promotions, Amazon can forecast increased demand for specific products based on historical data and customer browsing patterns. By leveraging AI in demand forecasting, Amazon adjusts its inventory levels accordingly, ensuring adequate stock availability to meet customer demand while minimizing excess inventory that ties up capital and increases carrying costs.

The benefits of AI-driven demand forecasting extend beyond just maintaining optimal inventory levels. Companies can use these insights to make more informed decisions regarding production scheduling, purchasing, and even pricing strategies. For instance, if the AI system predicts a surge in demand for a particular product, you can adjust production schedules or negotiate favorable terms with suppliers in preparation for the anticipated increase in demand.

Additionally, AI-powered demand forecasting can help organizations identify emerging trends and adapt their product offerings accordingly. By analyzing social media sentiments, customer reviews, and market trends, you can spot changing consumer preferences and adjust their inventory mix. This proactive approach enables organizations to stay ahead of the curve and meet customer expectations, boosting customer satisfaction and loyalty.

However, it's important to note that AI is not infallible, and demand forecasting may still face uncertainties and unexpected fluctuations. External factors like political events, natural disasters, or sudden shifts in consumer behavior can influence demand patterns beyond what historical or social media data can predict. Therefore, companies must not solely rely on AI-generated forecasts but should also incorporate human judgment and real-time market intelligence to make informed decisions.

However, by harnessing the power of AI in demand forecasting, organizations can optimize their inventory management practices and achieve several benefits. These include reducing stock-outs, minimizing excess inventory and associated costs, enabling proactive decision-making, and enhancing customer satisfaction. The remarkable efficiency and order fulfillment rate demonstrated by Amazon's AI-driven inventory management system serve as a perfect example of how effective demand forecast can significantly impact business performance.

Process Automation

Process automation is a key area where AI can drastically improve inventory management. By leveraging AI technologies, organizations can automate repetitive and time-consuming tasks involved in inventory tracking, supply chain optimization, and order fulfillment. This not only reduces the risk of human error but also enables employees to focus on more strategic activities, ultimately leading to improved efficiency and reduced operational costs.

One prominent example of AI-driven process automation in inventory management is Alibaba, one of the world's largest e-commerce companies. Alibaba utilizes AI extensively in its inventory management system to automate various tasks, including real-time inventory tracking. As sales occur, the AI system automatically updates inventory levels, ensuring accurate and up-to-date information.

With real-time inventory tracking, Alibaba can streamline its purchasing processes by having clear visibility of stock levels and automatically placing orders to restock when inventory reaches a certain threshold. This proactive approach to inventory management minimizes the risk of stockouts and improves order fulfillment rates. Additionally, the system allows Alibaba to provide customers with accurate and reliable order fulfillment estimates, enhancing the overall customer experience.

Furthermore, AI-powered process automation in inventory management extends beyond inventory tracking. By analyzing historical data, supplier performance, lead times, and market trends, the AI system can optimize supply chain logistics, helping you minimize costs and improve operational efficiency.

For example, Alibaba's AI system can intelligently forecast demand based on customer behavior and market trends. This information allows them to optimize their supply chain by identifying the most cost-effective transportation routes, reducing lead times, and ensuring the right products are available at the right locations. By automating these processes, Alibaba can improve its operational efficiency, deliver products faster, and ultimately provide better customer service.

However, it's important to consider the limitations of process automation through AI. While AI systems can perform tasks with speed and precision, they may struggle to adapt to unforeseen circumstances or handle complex scenarios that require human judgment. Human oversight and intervention remain crucial to ensure that AI-generated outputs align with business goals and address unique situations.

Overall, though, AI-driven process automation in inventory management offers significant benefits to organizations. By automating tasks such as inventory tracking, supply chain optimization, and order fulfillment, businesses can reduce errors, improve efficiency, and lower operational costs. Alibaba's AI-powered inventory management system serves as a prime example, demonstrating how automation can enable real-time inventory tracking, streamline purchasing processes, and enhance customer satisfaction. As organizations continue to leverage AI technologies, they can unlock the full potential of process automation in inventory management to gain a competitive advantage in the market.

Optimal Inventory Control

Optimal inventory control is crucial for organizations to minimize carrying costs and improve overall profitability. AI algorithms play a vital role in analyzing enormous volumes of data to identify the ideal inventory levels at various stages of the supply chain. By leveraging AI in inventory control, companies can reduce excess inventory while ensuring adequate stock availability, leading to optimized cash flow and increased operational efficiency.

One of the prime examples of AI-enabled optimal inventory control is Walmart. As one of the largest retail chains globally, Walmart utilizes AI extensively in its inventory management system. The AI system continuously monitors sales patterns, market trends, and customer behaviors to make data-driven decisions regarding pricing, promotions, and replenishment.

Through AI analysis, Walmart can accurately predict demand for products at different locations and adjust their inventory levels accordingly. This ensures that stores have sufficient stock to meet customer demand while minimizing overstocking. By achieving the optimal balance between inventory levels and customer demand, Walmart not only reduces stockouts – which improves customer satisfaction – but also avoids the costs associated with excess inventory.

Furthermore, AI algorithms contribute to efficient replenishment processes. The system can forecast when stock levels will reach reorder points and automatically generate purchase orders or trigger alerts for manual intervention. This proactive approach aids in avoiding stockouts and ensures a smooth flow of products through the supply chain.

However, it is important to note that AI algorithms for optimal inventory control require accurate and relevant data inputs. Organizations should continuously monitor the quality and integrity of data sources to ensure accurate demand forecasting and inventory optimization.

Overall, AI-powered optimal inventory control provides significant benefits to organizations by minimizing excess inventory, reducing carrying costs, and improving cash flow. Walmart's AI-enabled inventory management system serves as an excellent illustration of the advantages gained through accurate demand forecasting, dynamic pricing, and efficient replenishment processes. By leveraging AI in inventory control, you can achieve operational excellence, increase customer satisfaction, and drive overall profitability.

Risks and Challenges

While AI has the potential to significantly improve inventory management, its implementation comes with inherent risks and challenges that organizations need to be aware of and mitigate effectively. It is important to recognize and address these risks to ensure successful AI integration and minimize potential negative impacts. Let's delve into the main risks and challenges associated with AI in inventory management:

Data Quality and Integration

Data quality and integration are critical factors for the successful implementation of AI in inventory management. High-quality data ensures that AI algorithms generate accurate and reliable insights, allowing organizations to make informed decisions regarding inventory optimization and supply chain management. Here's an in-depth exploration of data quality and integration in the context of AI for inventory management.

Data Quality Assurance:

Organizations must establish robust data quality control processes to ensure the accuracy, completeness, and integrity of the data used for AI analysis. Some key steps to ensure data quality include:

- Data Cleansing: Regularly audit and clean the data to eliminate errors, duplicates, and inconsistent values. This process helps maintain data accuracy and integrity, reducing the risk of faulty AI outputs.
- Data Validation: Implement processes to validate data accuracy and completeness at the point of entry and during integration. By validating data against predefined rules and standards, organizations can identify and rectify data issues promptly.

- Data Governance: Define and enforce data governance policies that outline data quality standards, data ownership, and maintenance responsibilities. This ensures accountability for data accuracy and promotes a culture of data-driven decision-making.
- Data Documentation: Properly document data sources, transformations, and cleaning processes. Transparent documentation enhances the traceability and reliability of data, enabling better understanding and auditing of AI models.

Data Integration:

Data integration is crucial for AI systems to access and consolidate data from various sources within the organization. This integration allows for a unified and comprehensive view of inventory across the supply chain. Some considerations for effective data integration include:

- Unified Data Architecture: Create a standardized data architecture that facilitates the integration of data from disparate sources, such as sales systems, supplier databases, inventory management platforms, and market trend data. Well-designed data integration frameworks streamline data access and facilitate data sharing across systems.
- Data Mapping and Transformation: Employ data mapping and transformation techniques to ensure seamless integration of data from various systems. This involves aligning data fields and formats to ensure consistency and compatibility between different datasets.
- Real-time Data Integration: Implement real-time data integration processes to enable timely access to data from different sources. This allows organizations to leverage up-to-date information for accurate demand forecasting, inventory tracking, and replenishment decisions.
- Advanced Analytics: Explore advanced analytics techniques, such as data lakes or data warehouses, to store and analyze large volumes of integrated data. These technologies provide a scalable infrastructure for AI algorithms to process and generate insights from diverse datasets.

By prioritizing data quality assurance and effective data integration, organizations can harness the full potential of AI in inventory management. Accurate and integrated data provides a solid foundation for AI algorithms, enabling enhanced demand forecasting, optimized inventory levels, improved supply chain efficiency, and ultimately, better business outcomes.

Implementation Costs

Implementing AI systems for inventory management involves upfront costs related to infrastructure, software, and skilled personnel. These costs can present challenges, particularly for small and medium-sized businesses. However, with careful planning and a thorough cost-benefit analysis, organizations can justify the investment in AI and identify key areas where it can have the most significant impact. Let's explore these aspects in more detail:

Infrastructure Costs

AI implementation typically requires robust computational resources to handle the processing and analysis of large datasets. This may involve investing in servers, data storage facilities, cloud computing services, and networking infrastructure. The costs associated with acquiring and maintaining these infrastructure components should be considered during the planning stage.

Cloud-based solutions are often an attractive option for organizations looking to implement AI systems with reduced upfront infrastructure costs. Cloud providers offer scalable resources, allowing you to pay for what you use, reducing the need for substantial initial investments.

Software Costs

AI software is a crucial element of implementing AI systems. It includes tools for data analysis, machine learning models, and AI algorithms. The costs may involve licensing fees, subscription fees for cloud-based AI platforms, or custom development costs if bespoke solutions are required.

When evaluating AI software options, organizations should consider factors such as features, scalability, ease of integration with existing systems, vendor support, and long-term sustainability.

Skilled Personnel

Implementing and maintaining AI systems require skilled personnel, including data scientists, AI engineers, and domain experts. However, it can be costly to hire or train personnel with AI expertise, especially considering the demand for, and scarcity of, AI talent in the job market.

Instead, you have options for building AI capabilities in your teams. You can hire experienced professionals, partner with AI consultancy firms, or provide training and development programs to upskill existing employees. Careful consideration should be given to aligning AI talent requirements with your organization's overall AI strategy and long-term goals.

Cost-Benefit Analysis

Conducting a thorough cost-benefit analysis is crucial to assess the potential return on investment (ROI) of AI implementation in inventory management. This analysis should include factors such as:

- Cost savings from optimized inventory levels, reduced stockouts, and improved supply chain efficiency.
- Potential revenue growth resulting from enhanced demand forecasting, higher customer satisfaction, and improved product availability.
- Operational efficiency gains through process automation, reducing manual labor costs and reallocating employee time to more strategic tasks.
- Competitive advantages gained through improved decision-making and agility in responding to market dynamics.

By quantifying the benefits and comparing them to the implementation costs, organizations can make informed decisions on the viability and prioritization of AI projects in inventory management.

It is important to note that AI implementation costs can vary depending on the scale and complexity of your operations. Small and medium-sized businesses may focus on starting with smaller, targeted AI projects that offer immediate benefits and allow for iterative growth with the organization's resources and capabilities.

Overall, however, by conducting a comprehensive cost-benefit analysis, you can assess the affordability and potential impact of implementing AI systems for inventory management. This analysis helps in justifying the investment, identifying areas to prioritize, and ensuring the best use of resources to achieve significant improvements in inventory optimization, supply chain efficiency, and overall business performance.

Overreliance on AI

While AI algorithms provide valuable insights and automate various aspects of inventory management, organizations must be cautious of overreliance on AI without incorporating human judgment and expertise. While AI systems excel in analyzing large datasets and making accurate predictions based on historical patterns, they may not fully account for contextual nuances and unexpected events that can impact inventory needs. It is critical to strike a balance between AI capabilities and human oversight to ensure effective decision-making. Here are some key considerations for managing the risk of overreliance on AI in inventory management:

1. Contextual Understanding: Human expertise and domain knowledge are essential for contextualizing AI outputs. While AI algorithms excel in analyzing data, humans bring a nuanced understanding of the market, customer behavior, and subtle factors that may not be captured within the datasets. By combining AI-generated insights with human judgment, organizations can make more robust decisions regarding inventory optimization and supply chain management.

2. Validation and Verification: Organizations should establish validation processes to evaluate and verify AI outputs. This includes monitoring AI performance, comparing predictions with ground truth data, and regularly reviewing the accuracy and reliability of AI-generated insights. Human oversight can identify any anomalies, validate models against real-world scenarios, and make necessary adjustments to enhance accuracy and ensure the AI system aligns with your business goals.

3. Exception Handling and Adaptability: AI systems may struggle to handle unique situations and unforeseen events. Organizations should define protocols for handling exceptions and outliers that fall outside the scope of AI algorithms' predictions. Human experts should be involved in monitoring for situational changes, making timely adjustments to inventory levels, and ensuring responsiveness to unpredictable market dynamics.

4. Continuous Learning and Improvement: AI algorithms can adapt to changing patterns, but they require regular updates and improvements to remain effective. Organizations should continuously monitor and assess the performance of AI models, leveraging human insights to identify areas for refinement and enhancing the AI system's capabilities. By combining the power of AI and human insights, you can continuously refine your inventory management strategies and respond effectively to evolving market demands.

5. Collaborative Decision-Making: Foster collaboration between AI experts, data scientists, and inventory management professionals. By integrating diverse perspectives, you can achieve a comprehensive and well-rounded approach to decision-making. This collaborative environment cultivates continuous learning and knowledge sharing, allowing for more effective and ethical use of AI in inventory management.

By maintaining a balance between AI capabilities and human judgment, organizations can achieve better risk management, maintain control over their inventory management strategies, and ensure that AI-driven decisions align with broader business goals and strategies. The combination of AI and human expertise will contribute to more nuanced decision-making, improved responsiveness to changing market dynamics, and ultimately, optimized inventory control.

To effectively address the risks and challenges associated with AI in inventory management, organizations can implement the following strategies:

Data Quality Assurance:

Establish data quality control processes to ensure accurate, complete, and reliable data. Regularly audit and clean data to minimize errors and discrepancies that can negatively impact AI-driven inventory management decisions. Implement data governance practices, such as standardized data entry protocols and data validation checks, to maintain data integrity.

Robust Data Integration:

Invest in data integration to consolidate data from various sources and systems within the organization. This ensures a unified view of inventory across the supply chain, facilitating accurate demand forecasting and inventory optimization. Establish data mapping frameworks and data integration platforms to streamline data flow and maintain data consistency.

Scalable Infrastructure:

Adopt scalable AI infrastructure that can accommodate the growing volume of data and evolving business needs. This ensures that AI systems can continue to generate accurate and timely insights as your organization expands. Cloud-based solutions can provide flexibility and scalability, enabling efficient data processing and analysis without extensive upfront infrastructure costs.

Skill and Knowledge Development:

Invest in training and upskilling employees to understand AI concepts, interpret AI-generated insights, and effectively leverage AI for inventory management decisions. Collaborate with data scientists, AI experts, and inventory management professionals to bridge the gap between technical AI knowledge and operational expertise. Foster a culture of continuous learning and knowledge sharing within your organization.

Continuous Monitoring and Improvement:

Regularly monitor the performance of AI systems, evaluate key inventory metrics, and gather feedback from inventory managers and frontline employees. Assess the accuracy and reliability of AI-generated insights against real-world outcomes and make necessary adjustments to optimize inventory management processes. Continually evaluate data quality and the performance of AI models to ensure ongoing improvements and effectiveness.

By proactively implementing these strategies, you can mitigate risks and overcome challenges associated with AI in inventory management. You can leverage AI's capabilities to achieve operational excellence, improve customer satisfaction, and gain a competitive advantage in the market. Continuous monitoring and improvement will ensure that the AI systems remain effective and aligned with your evolving business needs and objectives.

Conclusion

In conclusion, the integration of Artificial Intelligence (AI) into inventory management has the potential to revolutionize supply chain operations and drive significant business growth. AI tools offer numerous benefits, including accurate demand forecasting, process automation, and optimal inventory control. By leveraging these capabilities, organizations can achieve remarkable efficiency gains, cost savings, and improved customer satisfaction.

However, it is important to acknowledge and address the risks and challenges that come with AI implementation. Data quality assurance is crucial to ensure accurate and reliable insights. Organizations must establish data quality control processes and invest in data integration capabilities to ensure the seamless flow of data across different platforms and systems. Moreover, implementation costs can be a barrier, particularly for smaller businesses. A thorough cost-benefit analysis is essential to justify the investment and identify the areas where AI will have the most substantial impact.

Additionally, overreliance on AI can pose risks. While AI algorithms demonstrate high accuracy, they may not account for sudden shifts in customer behavior, market dynamics, or unforeseen external events. Striking the right balance between AI capabilities and human judgment is crucial. Human oversight and expertise are necessary to validate AI outputs, make exceptions for unique situations, and ensure that AI-driven decisions align with business goals and strategies.

To successfully implement AI in inventory management, organizations should follow a well-formed plan. This includes implementing strategies for data quality assurance, robust data integration, scalable infrastructure, skill development, and continuous monitoring and improvement. By proactively addressing risks, leveraging AI tools, and emphasizing collaboration between teams, you can unlock the full potential of AI in inventory management.

The time to embrace AI in inventory management is now. Organizations that leverage AI technologies will gain a competitive advantage in today's fast-paced and data-driven business landscape. By harnessing the power of AI for demand forecasting, process automation, and optimal inventory control, companies can achieve operational excellence, improve customer satisfaction, and ultimately drive business success in an ever-evolving market.

GPT as Your Personal Assistant

Introduction

In the age of cutting-edge technology, we constantly seek ways to simplify and enhance our daily tasks. Artificial Intelligence (AI) has evolved to the point where it can now help us tackle various challenges. One remarkable application of AI technology, particularly GPT (Generative Pretrained Transformer) models, is transforming how we approach personal assistance. In this chapter, we will explore the myriad ways GPT technology can be configured as a personal assistant to revolutionize your productivity.

What is GPT?

Generative Pretrained Transformers, or GPT, are a class of AI models designed to generate human-like text based on given prompts. These models are built using deep learning techniques and can understand context, generating coherent and contextually relevant responses. GPT models have been pre-trained on vast amounts of internet text data, making them capable of assisting with a wide array of tasks.

Configuring GPT as Your Personal Assistant

To harness GPT as a personal assistant, you need to follow a few configuration steps

1. Select a GPT model: When configuring GPT as your personal assistant, it is crucial to choose the right model that aligns with your needs. Consider factors such as the size of the model, the training data it was pretrained on, and any specialized features it offers. For

example, if you require your assistant to handle complex language translations, you may opt for a model that has been fine-tuned for multilingual tasks. Conversely, if you only need basic text generation capabilities, a smaller, more lightweight model may suffice.

2. Set up a runtime environment: GPT models require significant computational resources to function optimally. Running these models locally can be challenging unless you have access to powerful hardware with sufficient memory and processing capabilities. To overcome this hurdle, consider utilizing cloud-based solutions like Google Colaboratory, which offer free access to GPU resources, or dedicated AI platforms like OpenAI, which provide preconfigured environments for running GPT models efficiently.

3. Define your assistant's capabilities: To make the most of your GPT-powered assistant, you need to define the specific tasks and functionalities you want it to handle. By explicitly guiding the model during interactions, you can shape its responses to suit your requirements. For instance, if you want your assistant to prioritize providing concise summaries, you can fine-tune the model on summarization-specific datasets. This will enable your assistant to generate more accurate and concise summaries. Defining your assistant's capabilities helps tailor its responses to be more relevant, accurate, and appropriate for the specific tasks you assign it.

4. Establish a feedback loop: When configuring GPT as your personal assistant, remember that it is essential to continuously provide feedback to the model. By providing explicit feedback, corrections, or suggestions, you can train the model to improve its responses over time. This feedback loop is critical for fine-tuning the assistant to understand your preferences, writing style, and the specific nuances of your demands. Regularly refining and updating the assistant's training data using user feedback ensures that it continually adapts and learns to provide a better user experience.

5. Ensure privacy and data security: As with any AI assistant, it is important to prioritize privacy and data security. When configuring GPT as your personal assistant, ensure that sensitive information and personal data are handled securely. Avoid storing private data within the model or the runtime environment. If utilizing cloud-based platforms, review their privacy policies to understand how your data is stored and protected. By taking the necessary precautions, you can confidently use GPT technology as your personal assistant while safeguarding your personal information.

Following these configuration steps optimizes GPT as your personal assistant, enabling it to handle your desired tasks effectively and efficiently. Moreover, by selecting the right model, setting up an appropriate runtime environment, defining your assistant's capabilities, establishing a feedback loop, and ensuring data security, you can seamlessly integrate GPT technology into your daily routine, enhancing your productivity and simplifying your tasks.

Tasks GPT Can Perform as Your Personal Assistant

1. Natural Language Processing and Understanding: GPT models excel at understanding and generating human-like text, making them ideal for tasks involving natural language processing. As a personal assistant, GPT can assist you in a conversational manner by answering questions, providing explanations, and summarizing long documents. Whether you need to know the capital of a country or understand a complex concept, GPT can process and generate coherent responses that mimic human understanding.

2. Managing Emails and Scheduling: With its natural language capabilities, GPT can help you efficiently manage your inbox and schedule. It can filter emails based on specified criteria, categorize them, and even draft responses to routine queries. GPT can integrate seamlessly with your calendar, enabling it to schedule appointments, set reminders, and organize your daily agenda. By delegating these repetitive tasks to your GPT assistant, you can save time and focus on more important matters.

3. Research and Information Gathering: GPT assistants excel at research tasks, making them invaluable aids for gathering information. Whether you need to quickly find information on a specific topic or dive deep into research papers, GPT can quickly crawl vast amounts of data and provide relevant summaries or sources for further reading. This capability not only saves you time but also ensures that you have accurate and useful information at your fingertips.

4. Language Translation: Language barriers can hinder effective communication, but with GPT as your personal assistant, you can overcome this challenge. By configuring GPT as a language translator, you can facilitate seamless communication across various languages. GPT can translate text or even help you in real-time conversations. For frequent travelers or multi-lingual communicators, this feature can be immensely valuable, enabling you to connect with people from different cultures and backgrounds effortlessly.

5. Personalized Assistant: GPT can be trained on your personal data to create a personalized assistant experience. By providing it with information such as your preferences, interests, or writing style, GPT can offer tailored suggestions, recommendations or even generate content that aligns with your unique needs. This personalized touch enhances the user experience and ensures that your assistant understands you better over time. Whether it's suggesting books based on your favorite genres or composing emails in your writing style, the personalized assistant aspect of GPT can truly make it feel like an indispensable companion.

GPT technology, when configured as a personal assistant, can perform a wide range of tasks with exceptional proficiency. From natural language processing and understanding to managing emails and scheduling, GPT can streamline your workflow and enhance your productivity. Its research capabilities, language translation functions, and personalized assistant features further contribute to its value as a comprehensive AI-powered personal assistant. When you harness GPT technology, you empower yourself with an efficient and reliable assistant that understands and caters to your unique needs.

Conclusion

In conclusion, harnessing GPT technology as your personal assistant brings remarkable benefits to enhance your productivity and streamline your day-to-day tasks. The range of capabilities inherent in GPT models makes them an indispensable tool for various functions. By selecting the right GPT model, setting up a suitable runtime environment, defining your assistant's capabilities, establishing a feedback loop, and ensuring data security, you can optimize the use of GPT as your personal assistant.

GPT excels in natural language processing and understanding, allowing it to answer questions, provide explanations, and summarize documents in a conversational manner. Its email and scheduling management abilities enable efficient organization, filtering, and drafting of responses, saving valuable time. By utilizing GPT for research and information gathering, you gain access to vast amounts of data, allowing for quick information retrieval and quality summaries. GPT's language translation capabilities bridge communication gaps, making it an invaluable tool for overcoming language barriers. Additionally, trained on personal data, GPT can offer personalized assistance, tailoring its suggestions, recommendations, and content generation to better suit your unique preferences and needs.

Overall, embracing GPT technology as your personal assistant enables you to optimize your efficiency, delegate routine tasks, and leverage the power of AI in your daily routine. Communication becomes more convenient, research becomes more comprehensive, and language barriers become surmountable. Harnessing GPT technology empowers you with a versatile and reliable assistant that understands and adapts to your specific requirements.

Ultimately, the integration of GPT technology as your personal assistant brings a significant shift in how you approach your tasks. It streamlines your workflow, enhances your productivity, and allows you to focus on the aspects that truly matter. Embrace the potential of AI and transform your daily routine by harnessing GPT technology as your trusted personal assistant.

General AI: Impacts on Business, Society, and Humanity

THE RAPID EVOLUTION OF ARTIFICIAL INTELLIGENCE over the past decade has been breathtaking. Systems can now outmatch humans at games like chess and Go, understand natural language, translate between languages, caption images and make predictions based on large volumes of data. However, current AI systems are narrow in scope, focused on excelling at specific, pre-defined tasks.

The next frontier in AI development is achieving Artificial General Intelligence (AGI) – flexible, human-level AI systems that possess general problem-solving capabilities and can adapt to a wide range of environments and challenges. AGI remains on the horizon, but steady progress in algorithms, computing power, and troves of data put its advent within reach. When realized, AGI has the potential to revolutionize corporations, turbocharge productivity, and transform society.

Defining the Hallmarks of Artificial General Intelligence

Artificial General Intelligence refers to machines with cognitive abilities at or beyond the human level. This entails features such as:

- Understanding and using natural language, including comprehension of linguistic nuances like metaphors and humor.
- Learning and applying knowledge gained in one domain to other novel domains. For instance, recognizing that the strategies used to win a game could be applied when making business decisions.
- Recognizing patterns and making logical inferences from limited data, handling uncertainty and ambiguity with rational thought.

- Formulating original ideas and demonstrating creativity and imagination. Coming up with novel solutions to problems.
- Showing reasoning capabilities across multiple modalities such as visual, textual, auditory, and sensor-based inputs.
- Developing subjective experiences, self-awareness, and sentience.

AGI systems display broad capabilities across intellectual domains, similar to gifted polymaths. They acquire new skills and knowledge to handle unfamiliar tasks and environments. In contrast, today's AI systems excel in narrow domains but cannot transfer learning to generalize across multiple areas.

Current Approaches to Realizing AGI

Many techniques are being explored to achieve the complex general intelligence exhibited by humans:

- Advanced neural networks that mimic the architecture of the human brain through artificial neurons and dynamic neural connections. Models like deep learning have achieved impressive results on narrow tasks. Research is ongoing on extending these to general problem-solving.
- Computational models of reasoning that explicitly represent knowledge and logical rules, enabling logical deduction. Integrating these symbolic models with neural networks holds promise.
- Reinforcement learning, where systems learn through trial, error, and incremental reward. This builds up experiential knowledge akin to human learning.
- Hybrid systems that combine neural networks, logical reasoning, knowledge representation, and reinforcement learning. This provides complementary strengths of multiple approaches.
- Architecture development, including organizing modules and knowledge stores to replicate functional regions of the human brain. Architectural advances will be vital to realizing AGI.
- Self-supervised and unsupervised learning to generate knowledge from unlabeled data in a more human-like manner.
- Simulated environments and games to provide safe platforms for accumulating broadly-applicable learning.

- Studying neuroscience and cognitive science to reverse-engineer the algorithms underlying human intelligence.

Immense research still remains to integrate all these varied components into a system exhibiting the multi-faceted, flexible intelligence of the human mind. But AGI may be achieved through incremental advancements building on current AI, rather than one single eureka moment. With continued progress, AGI could move from speculative possibility to practical reality within our lifetimes.

Revolutionizing Business and Commerce

When realized, AGI promises to revolutionize nearly every facet of business operations and commerce. Some potential impacts include:

Strategic Decision Making

AGI systems could analyze massive sets of multi-modal data, recognize subtle patterns and make predictions to inform strategic business decisions. For example, an AGI could:

- Process volumes of consumer data to precisely model customer preferences and demand for upcoming products.
- Assess competitive landscape and market dynamics to predict optimal timing for entering new markets.
- Configure supply chains and logistics networks to cost-effectively meet demand based on sales forecasts.
- Scan news, social media, and political developments to assess public sentiment and reputation risks.
- Project climate change impacts on markets and natural resources that could disrupt operations or alter long-term plans.
- Forecast demographic shifts and their effects on the workforce and talent pipelines.

With such insights, leaders could make strategy calls with greater confidence, primed to capitalize on emerging opportunities.

Streamlined Operations

AGI could optimize and automate complex business operations:

- Adjust manufacturing pipelines and inventory in real-time based on supply constraints, equipment breakdowns, and changing priorities.
- Dynamically schedule staff and resources to maximize productivity and minimize costs.
- Provide real-time translation services for global companies and multi-lingual customers.
- Automate mundane administrative tasks like processing forms, invoices, and applications.
- Respond to customer inquiries quickly and accurately, regardless of language.
- Rapidly interpret troves of user data to fix software bugs before they impact customers.

By removing bottlenecks and smoothing workflows, AGI stands to unleash enormous gains in efficiency.

Enhanced Innovation

AGI systems could accelerate innovation cycles by:

- Rapidly analyzing decades of research papers and lab results to infer promising new hypotheses and experiments.
- Simulating millions of molecular interactions to reduce timeframes for developing new medicines or materials.
- Suggesting creative new design possibilities based on first principles and without human biases.
- Conceiving and prototyping novel patentable technologies.
- Providing designers and engineers an intuitive VR interface and real-time feedback to refine prototypes.

These abilities could compress R&D timelines down to a fraction of what is possible today, enabling an explosion of transformative new products and services.

Societal and Ethics Considerations

To minimize risks and build trust, AGI systems must incorporate ethics and align with human values from the outset:

- Protect privacy by limiting data collection, enabling opt-outs, and anonymizing user data.
- Ensure transparency by having humans set objectives and audit algorithms.
- Minimize bias by testing systems for unwanted discrimination and prejudicial decisions.
- Implement oversight measures like human monitoring and control of emergency stop buttons.
- Set explicit constraints on harmful actions and embed human rights into goal structures.
- Develop techniques for value alignment, where AGI absorbs ethical norms through observation and learning.

With thoughtful design, AGI could help address global challenges like inequality, poverty and climate change, improving life for all humans. We must proactively shape its emergence to maximize the chance of beneficial outcomes.

Transforming the Nature of Work

The economic transitions spurred by AGI will also profoundly reshape the employment landscape. Some developments include:

- Automating rote and routine physical and cognitive jobs. Manufacturing, data entry, bookkeeping, clerical work, and quality monitoring could be handled 24/7 by AGI.
- Complementing and augmenting human capabilities. Exoskeletons could enable manual workers to lift more. AGI assistants could perform tedious tasks and free up human creative potential.
- Changing skill demands. As routine jobs are automated, uniquely human skills like creativity, empathy, collaboration, communication, and entrepreneurship will be increasingly valued. Lifelong learning to acquire new skills will be critical.
- Emerging roles and sectors. New jobs will arise in areas like AGI development, oversight, ethics, and regulation. Entirely new industries could flourish under the technological upheaval of AGI.

- Job displacement hardships. For workers replaced by automation, income support, retraining programs, and educational initiatives will be essential to ease the transition and avoid societal ruptures.
- The end of work? In a hypothetical scenario where AGI exceeds human capabilities across virtually all tasks, human labor may no longer be required. This could require a fundamental rethinking of economics, with concepts like universal basic income gaining prominence.

With planning, education, and support, this workforce transformation can unlock new opportunities and more meaningful work.

Boosting Human Productivity

AGI promises to unlock enormous gains in human productivity:

- Alleviating drudgery by automating mundane, repetitive tasks. Offloading dull work to AGI systems will allow people to focus on creative, interpersonal, and strategic endeavors.
- Augmenting human abilities. Exoskeletons and implants could enhance strength, precision, stamina, and recall. Intelligent assistants could help people think, learn, and make decisions.
- Personalized education. AGI tutors could provide customized training optimized for each student's strengths, weaknesses, interests, and learning methods. This can accelerate skill building.
- Medical insights. AGI could parse patient data to supply healthcare staff with diagnosis and treatment recommendations, boosting the quality of care. It could also enable personalized medicine.
- Scientific leaps. AGI's ability to rapidly synthesize research, hypothesize, simulate, and test could collapse R&D timelines across every scientific field.
- Creative stimulus. Exposure to AGI's novel innovations and unconventional strategies could expand human creative horizons and inspire new paradigms.

Rather than displacing humans, AGI can amplify our capabilities and achievements beyond what either can attain alone.

Societal Benefits

Thoughtfully implemented, AGI could help address many social challenges:

- Improving healthcare outcomes through rapid medical insights and personalized treatment plans.
- Democratizing access to education by customizing instruction for students everywhere based on individual needs.
- Optimizing transportation systems, logistics, and infrastructure planning to improve quality of life across communities.
- Early disease outbreak prediction and guidance for targeted intervention to contain infectious epidemics.
- Help balance production and distribution of food, water, clean energy, and other resources to improve sustainable development.
- Automating unpleasant tasks to free up time for recreational, social, and creative pursuits, facilitating self-actualization.
- Providing fulfilling opportunities for the elderly and disabled by intelligently augmenting their capabilities.

An abundance mindset sees AGI as expanding the frontier of human potential and flourishing. With ethical foundations, its benefits could touch lives globally.

The Road Ahead

The full promise and risks of AGI remain uncertain. It may arrive sooner through an unexpected breakthrough or remain distant. Technical obstacles and funding challenges may slow progress. Regardless, wise preparation and planning are prudent to steer AGI toward augmenting human potential and away from misuse.

No technology as profoundly powerful as AGI has ever been developed. It represents a threshold moment in human history, rife with opportunity to lift humanity to new heights. But without caution, AGI could exacerbate existing problems or create new catastrophes. People across nations, generations and demographics will be impacted on sweeping scales. Inclusive public dialog and collaboration is imperative to navigate the road ahead responsibly and beneficially.

With vision and compassion, we can shape AGI as a stepping stone to a future of safety, justice, creativity, and human flourishing. It could launch a new Renaissance – allowing discovery, invention, and culture to thrive beyond what is possible today. But we must be proactive in embedding ethics, cementing human values, and designing appropriate oversight up front in AGI architectures. If developed thoughtfully, this remarkable technology could help humanity transcend limits and fulfill our vast latent promise.

Impacts on Executives and Managers

The emergence of AGI stands to profoundly impact corporate executives and line managers. With preparation, however, they can harness AGI capabilities to enhance decision-making, streamline operations, and unlock human potential.

Strategic Foresight

Rather than relying solely on intuition, executives could tap AGI systems to inject data-driven foresight into strategy:

- AGI could rapidly analyze news, financial data, demographics, political developments, and other factors to assess risks, competitive threats, and growth opportunities.
- Scenario planning simulations could allow executives to stress test strategic plans against thousands of possible futures.
- By considering perspectives beyond human biases, AGI may uncover strategic options that executives had not contemplated.

Management Augmentation

AGI could work alongside managers as an intelligent assistant:

- Reviewing customer, product, and employee data for insights on improving quality, culture, and efficiency. Human managers have limited time to parse such volumes of information.
- Monitoring workflows, collaboration, and performance to provide personalized coaching and staff development recommendations.

- Handling scheduling, event planning, and coordinating across departments – administrative tasks that can constrain managers' time and focus.
- Serving as a mentor that shares knowledge and teaches new skills on demand to get managers up to speed in evolving roles.

Objectivity and Bias Reduction

By design, AGI systems could counteract biases that often distort human decision-making:

- Reviewing performance data and assessments to flag biased evaluations or inconsistent application of standards across groups.
- Scanning hiring practices and personnel data to identify areas where diversity, equity, and inclusion programs need bolstering.
- Detecting past cases where cognitive biases affected sound judgement. Although algorithmic biases remain an ongoing challenge as well.
- Institutionalizing ethical frameworks, constraints on harmful actions, and monitoring mechanisms to steer AGI systems away from harmful biases.

Shared Human-AGI Management

Rather than wholesale replacement of management roles by AGI, humans and machines could each play to their complementary strengths:

- AGI handles data-intensive forecasting, prediction, analysis, and optimization.
- Humans manage interpersonal relationships, provide emotional intelligence, make nuanced ethical judgements, and set strategic priorities.
- Hybrid teams fuse human creativity, empathy, and values with AGI's speed, scalability, and objectivity.

Proactive Planning

To harness AGI's opportunities while mitigating risks, managers should:

- Invite technical experts to explain AGI's evolving capabilities and limitations in an accessible manner to their teams. Dispelling hype and fear will ground discussions.
- Explore pilot projects matching core problems with emerging AGI tools to gather hands-on experience.
- Survey employees to gauge expectations and concerns on AI-human collaboration, workforce transitions, privacy, and algorithmic bias. Share plans transparently.
- Review training programs and progress toward diversity, equity, and inclusion goals to prepare the organization for epic workplace changes.
- Follow AGI advances at leading research institutions to identify proven best practices and cautions against overhype.

Historic Leap for Business and Society

AGI represents an unprecedented technological shift, poised to transform corporations, accelerate innovation, and unlock human potential and flourishing. With inclusive ethics-focused preparation, its benefits could positively impact lives across the planet. However, risk factors like job displacement, algorithmic biases, and existential threats will require mitigation. Overall, business leaders have much to gain by proactively shaping AGI's emergence. Vision, compassion, and responsibility will light the way to amazing possibilities ahead.

The Path Forward

The emergence of Artificial General Intelligence represents a historic inflection point, poised to profoundly transform business and society. AGI has immense potential to accelerate innovation, improve decision-making, boost productivity, and address global problems – if developed responsibly and directed judiciously. However, risks around economic disruption, algorithmic bias, privacy erosion, and existential threats also loom large. Navigating this transition well requires proactive planning, ethical foundations, and wise governance.

Businesses stand to gain tremendously by incorporating AGI capabilities across operations and strategy. But leaders must simultaneously monitor impacts on workers, customers, and communities. Fostering public trust through transparency will prove critical. Managers at all levels need realistic timelines for adoption to update skills training, workflow redesign and diversity programs ahead of disruption waves. Governments cannot cling to outdated policy frameworks. Updated regulations on issues like data rights, AI safety, and accountability are needed to steer emerging technologies towards human betterment.

International coordination is also key, as AGI's impact spans geographic borders. Inclusive public discourse can help align development and deployment with shared human values. Beyond business, the scientific community, too, bears great responsibility. Multidisciplinary collaboration and institutional mechanisms for safety research are imperative. We must continue studying means of ensuring advanced AI behaves ethically and remains under meaningful human direction.

The choices we make today will steer the trajectory of societal impacts. With wisdom and empathy, we can shape AGI as a stepping stone to a brighter future – one where human virtues and potential flourish rather than fade; where human thinking is augmented rather than replaced. Technological advancement is inevitable, but progress is not predestined. It is up to us to pursue scientific knowledge and its application towards just, compassionate ends that benefit all people. If we can surmount this historic challenge with vision and values intact, an amazing future awaits where both artificial and human intelligence harmoniously lift civilization to new heights.

Conclusion: The Transformative Power of AI in Corporations

THE REALM OF ARTIFICIAL INTELLIGENCE (AI) continues to expand and reshape various aspects of our world today. What was once confined to science fiction has become a groundbreaking reality. From self-driving cars and voice-activated personal assistants to recommendation algorithms and barcode scanners, AI technologies have seamlessly integrated into our everyday lives. In this book, we have explored the implementation of AI in corporations and its transformative potential.

The journey began with an exploration of AI's historical roots, tracing its origins from the conceptualization of automated machines to the development of machine learning and neural networks. We witnessed the milestones and breakthroughs that paved the way for AI's current form. Understanding the historical context provides us with a comprehensive overview of this revolutionary technology and its rise to prominence.

Implementing AI in the enterprise requires careful planning and execution. We've outlined a comprehensive guide for successfully integrating AI into corporations. The process began with defining clear business goals that align with the organization's broader strategy. This is essential for ensuring that AI initiatives address specific pain points and drive value.

Assessing readiness and capabilities is the next crucial step. Organizations must evaluate data availability, infrastructure, and workforce expertise. This assessment determines whether internal resources are sufficient or if external partnerships or consultants are needed. Identifying suitable AI use cases comes next, prioritizing applications that offer significant potential value or address critical pain points.

However, developing a robust data strategy is imperative for successful AI implementation. Organizations must identify data sources, assess data quality and accessibility, and address any governance or compliance concerns. Proper data governance ensures the upholding of privacy, security, and ethical considerations.

Once the groundwork is laid, organizations must decide whether to build or acquire AI solutions. By evaluating available options, including open-source frameworks, cloud-based platforms, or partnerships with AI technology providers, organizations can choose the most suitable approach based on cost, scalability, and customization requirements.

But before deploying AI solutions organization-wide, pilot testing and proof of concept are crucial. This allows organizations to validate the feasibility and impact of AI initiatives in a controlled environment. Feedback and key performance indicators are collected and used to refine the approach as needed.

Once success is achieved in pilot testing, organizations can proceed with the implementation and integration of AI solutions across the enterprise. A detailed implementation plan outlines timelines, milestones, and resource allocation. Smooth integration with existing systems and processes is essential to minimize disruptions and ensure a seamless transition.

However, implementing AI is not a one-time event; it is an ongoing process. Continuous monitoring and evaluation are necessary to measure the performance, impact, and return on investment of AI initiatives. Key performance indicators related to productivity, cost savings, customer satisfaction, and business outcomes must be regularly reviewed and refined to ensure optimal results.

Change management and employee training also play a critical role in AI implementation. Communicating the benefits of AI to the workforce and addressing any concerns or resistance is essential. Offering comprehensive training programs to upskill and reskill employees will foster a culture of continuous learning and ensure smooth collaboration between humans and AI systems.

We noted that keeping updated with AI advancements is vital to staying ahead of the curve. The field of AI is rapidly evolving, with new technologies and research emerging constantly. By participating in industry events, conferences, and webinars, organizations can gain insights from experts and thought leaders, allowing them to leverage new opportunities and maintain competitiveness.

The implementation of AI in corporations is clearly a journey that requires careful planning, strategy, and execution. AI technologies have the potential to enhance efficiency, improve decision-making, and drive innovation. And by defining clear business goals, assessing readiness, identifying suitable use cases, and following systematic approaches, organizations can successfully harness the power of AI.

It is important to remember, however, that AI is not a replacement for human intelligence, but a powerful tool that enhances human capabilities. Balancing the integration of AI technologies with the human touch is essential for successful implementation – AI should always be seen as an assistant, augmenting human expertise and creativity.

The transformative power of AI in corporations is vast. It will continue to shape the future of work. Embracing AI technologies opens up new horizons for organizations, unlocking opportunities for growth, efficiency, and innovation. By leveraging AI, corporations can not only navigate the complexities of the modern business landscape but also thrive in an increasingly dynamic and challenging world.

As we embark on this journey, we must always keep in mind the ethical considerations and responsibilities associated with AI. Ensuring transparency, privacy, and fairness in AI implementation is crucial to building trust with employees, customers, and society at large.

We believe that, by embracing AI technologies and implementing them thoughtfully, corporations can revolutionize their operations and achieve unprecedented success. The realm of AI is ever-evolving, and organizations that adapt and leverage these technologies will be at the forefront of innovation and growth in the years to come.

Index

J

K

L

M

N

P

R

T

V